1

AdTech Unleashed: Navigating the Future of Digital Advertising with AI, ML, and Data Science

Table of Contents

3

1. INTRODUCTION TO ADTECH IN 2024

In the ever-evolving landscape of digital advertising, technological advancements have continuously reshaped the way advertisers and publishers engage with their audiences. As we enter the year 2024, the realm of Advertising Technology (AdTech) stands at the precipice of unprecedented innovation and transformation. This chapter serves as an introductory exploration into the state of AdTech in 2024, delving into the key trends, challenges, and opportunities shaping the industry.

THE EVOLUTION OF ADTECH

The inception of AdTech can be traced back to the nascent stages of digital advertising, which emerged alongside the rapid expansion of the internet in the late 20th century. In its earliest forms, digital advertising was relatively rudimentary, consisting mainly of static banner ads displayed on websites. During this era, advertisers relied on basic targeting techniques, such as contextual keywords and user demographics, to deliver ads to relevant audiences.

As the internet continued to evolve and consumer behavior shifted, AdTech underwent a remarkable transformation. The advent of search engines like Google introduced new opportunities for advertisers to reach consumers at the point of intent, leveraging keywords and search queries to deliver targeted ads. This marked the beginning of more sophisticated targeting capabilities in digital advertising, laying the groundwork for the future evolution of AdTech.

The proliferation of social media platforms further revolutionized the digital advertising landscape, providing advertisers with unprecedented access to highly engaged audiences. Social media platforms introduced innovative ad formats, such as sponsored posts and native advertising, which seamlessly integrated with users' feeds and timelines. These platforms also leveraged user data and engagement metrics to refine targeting algorithms, enabling advertisers to deliver highly personalized and relevant ads to their target audiences.

Furthermore, the rise of programmatic advertising and real-time bidding (RTB) technologies ushered in a new era of automation and efficiency in digital advertising. Programmatic platforms enabled advertisers to purchase ad inventory in real-time, using algorithms to optimize bidding strategies and target specific audience segments with precision. This shift towards programmatic advertising democratized access to digital ad inventory, allowing advertisers of all sizes to participate in auctions and reach their desired audiences more effectively.

In parallel, advancements in data analytics and machine learning paved the way for more sophisticated targeting and optimization capabilities in AdTech. Machine learning algorithms enabled advertisers to analyze vast amounts of data, including user behavior, demographics, and contextual signals, to identify patterns and trends that could inform ad targeting and campaign optimization strategies. These AI-driven insights empowered advertisers to deliver more relevant and personalized ads, driving higher engagement and conversion rates.

Overall, the evolution of AdTech has been characterized by a relentless pursuit of innovation and optimization, driven by advancements in technology and shifts in consumer behavior. From its humble beginnings as static banner ads on websites to the dynamic and data-driven ecosystem of today, AdTech continues to evolve rapidly, shaping the future of digital advertising in profound and impactful ways.

Today, AdTech encompasses a vast ecosystem of tools, platforms, and methodologies designed to facilitate the creation, delivery, and optimization of digital advertising campaigns across various channels and formats. From programmatic advertising and real-time bidding to data-driven targeting and personalized content recommendation, AdTech has become increasingly sophisticated and data-driven, revolutionizing the way advertisers connect with their target audiences.

THE ROLE OF PRODUCT MANAGERS IN ADTECH

Within the dynamic and complex ecosystem of Advertising Technology (AdTech), Product Managers serve as the linchpin, orchestrating the development, enhancement, and optimization of AdTech platforms and products. Tasked with navigating the intersection of business objectives, user needs, and technological capabilities, Product Managers play a multifaceted role that is pivotal to the success and innovation of AdTech solutions.

At the core of their responsibilities, Product Managers act as strategic visionaries, aligning product development efforts with overarching business goals and market demands. They collaborate closely with stakeholders across the organization, including executives, marketers, engineers, and data scientists, to define product roadmaps, prioritize feature development, and ensure the timely delivery of high-quality solutions.

One of the primary functions of Product Managers in AdTech is to act as advocates for the end user, championing their needs and preferences throughout the product development lifecycle. By conducting thorough market research, user interviews, and usability testing, Product Managers gain valuable insights into user behavior, pain points, and desires, which inform product decisions and drive user-centric innovation.

Moreover, Product Managers are responsible for translating business requirements and market insights into actionable product requirements and specifications. They work closely with cross-functional teams of engineers, designers, and data scientists to transform concepts into tangible features and functionalities, ensuring that the final product meets both user needs and technical feasibility.

In addition to driving product development efforts, Product Managers in AdTech are also tasked with optimizing existing products to enhance their performance, usability, and value proposition. They analyze user feedback, usage metrics, and market trends to identify opportunities for improvement and innovation, guiding iterative updates and enhancements to the product over time.

Furthermore, Product Managers play a critical role in fostering collaboration and alignment across diverse teams and departments within the organization. They serve as the central point of communication and coordination, facilitating cross-functional collaboration and ensuring that everyone is aligned with the product vision, goals, and priorities.

The role of Product Managers in AdTech is multifaceted and strategic, encompassing responsibilities ranging from defining product strategy and roadmaps to driving execution and optimization. By serving as the bridge between business objectives, user needs, and technological capabilities, Product Managers play a pivotal role in shaping the future of AdTech and driving innovation in the digital advertising landscape.

In 2024, Product Managers in AdTech are faced with a myriad of challenges and opportunities. They must navigate the complexities of an ever-changing regulatory landscape, address growing concerns around data privacy and consumer protection, and keep pace with rapid technological advancements. Moreover, they are tasked with delivering innovative solutions that not only meet the needs of advertisers and publishers but also enhance the overall user experience and drive tangible business results.

KEY TRENDS AND CHALLENGES IN ADTECH

As we peer into the future of Advertising Technology (AdTech) in 2024, it becomes evident that the industry is on the cusp of profound transformation. Several key trends and challenges are poised to shape the AdTech landscape, influencing the way advertisers engage with their audiences and the strategies they employ to drive success. Let's delve deeper into these trends and challenges:

1. The Rise of AI, ML, and Data Science:
In 2024, Artificial Intelligence (AI), Machine Learning (ML), and Data Science are set to revolutionize AdTech, empowering advertisers with unprecedented capabilities for targeting, personalization, and optimization. AI-driven algorithms analyze vast amounts of data to uncover insights about consumer behavior, preferences, and intent, enabling advertisers to deliver more relevant and timely ads. Machine learning algorithms continuously learn and adapt to changing market dynamics, optimizing ad campaigns in real time to maximize performance and ROI. Data science techniques, such as predictive analytics and segmentation, provide advertisers with actionable insights to inform strategic decision-making and drive business growth.

2. Privacy and Data Protection:

Heightened concerns around data privacy and regulatory compliance are reshaping the AdTech landscape, prompting advertisers to adopt transparent and ethical data practices. In the wake of stringent data protection regulations such as GDPR and CCPA, advertisers are tasked with ensuring that their data collection, usage, and consent management practices adhere to regulatory standards and respect user privacy preferences. Advertisers must strike a delicate balance between delivering personalized ad experiences and safeguarding user data, navigating a complex regulatory landscape while maintaining consumer trust and confidence.

3. Omnichannel Advertising:

The proliferation of digital channels and devices has ushered in a new era of omnichannel advertising, where advertisers must engage consumers across multiple touchpoints and platforms seamlessly. In 2024, AdTech platforms are evolving to support omnichannel advertising strategies, enabling advertisers to deliver cohesive and consistent brand experiences across channels such as mobile, desktop, social media, and connected devices. Advertisers are leveraging advanced targeting and attribution capabilities to track user interactions across channels, optimize ad delivery strategies, and measure the impact of their campaigns holistically.

4. Emerging Technologies:

Innovations such as augmented reality (AR), virtual reality (VR), and voice search are driving new opportunities and challenges for AdTech in 2024. These emerging technologies offer immersive and interactive advertising experiences, allowing advertisers to engage consumers in innovative ways. However, integrating these technologies into AdTech platforms presents technical and creative challenges, requiring advertisers to adapt their strategies and capabilities accordingly. AdTech product development teams must stay abreast of emerging technologies, experimenting with new formats and channels to stay ahead of the curve and deliver cutting-edge ad experiences.

The future of AdTech in 2024 is marked by the convergence of AI, ML, and Data Science, the evolving landscape of privacy and data protection, the shift towards omnichannel advertising, and the opportunities presented by emerging technologies. Advertisers must navigate these trends and challenges strategically, leveraging technology and innovation to drive success and stay competitive in an increasingly complex and dynamic digital advertising ecosystem.

KEY TRENDS AND CHALLENGES IN ADTECH

As we peer into the future of Advertising Technology (AdTech) in 2024, it becomes evident that the industry is on the cusp of profound transformation. Several key trends and challenges are poised to shape the AdTech landscape, influencing the way advertisers engage with their audiences and the strategies they employ to drive success. Let's delve deeper into these trends and challenges:

1. The Rise of AI, ML, and Data Science:
In 2024, Artificial Intelligence (AI), Machine Learning (ML), and Data Science are set to revolutionize AdTech, empowering advertisers with unprecedented capabilities for targeting, personalization, and optimization. AI-driven algorithms analyze vast amounts of data to uncover insights about consumer behavior, preferences, and intent, enabling advertisers to deliver more relevant and timely ads. Machine learning algorithms continuously learn and adapt to changing market dynamics, optimizing ad campaigns in real time to maximize performance and ROI. Data science techniques,

such as predictive analytics and segmentation, provide advertisers with actionable insights to inform strategic decision-making and drive business growth.

2. Privacy and Data Protection:

Heightened concerns around data privacy and regulatory compliance are reshaping the AdTech landscape, prompting advertisers to adopt transparent and ethical data practices. In the wake of stringent data protection regulations such as GDPR and CCPA, advertisers are tasked with ensuring that their data collection, usage, and consent management practices adhere to regulatory standards and respect user privacy preferences. Advertisers must strike a delicate balance between delivering personalized ad experiences and safeguarding user data, navigating a complex regulatory landscape while maintaining consumer trust and confidence.

3. Omnichannel Advertising:

The proliferation of digital channels and devices has ushered in a new era of omnichannel advertising, where advertisers must engage consumers across multiple touchpoints and platforms seamlessly. In 2024, AdTech platforms are evolving to support omnichannel advertising strategies, enabling advertisers to deliver cohesive and consistent brand experiences across channels such as mobile, desktop, social media, and connected devices. Advertisers are leveraging advanced targeting and attribution capabilities to track user interactions across channels, optimize ad delivery strategies, and measure the impact of their campaigns holistically.

4. Emerging Technologies:

Innovations such as augmented reality (AR), virtual reality (VR), and voice search are driving new opportunities and challenges for AdTech in 2024. These emerging technologies offer immersive and interactive advertising experiences, allowing advertisers to engage consumers in innovative ways. However, integrating these technologies into AdTech platforms presents technical and creative challenges, requiring advertisers to adapt their strategies and capabilities accordingly. AdTech product development teams must stay abreast of emerging technologies, experimenting with new formats and channels to stay ahead of the curve and deliver cutting-edge ad experiences.

2. UNDERSTANDING AI, ML & DATA SCIENCE ROLE IN ADTECH

In the rapidly evolving landscape of Advertising Technology (AdTech), the integration of Artificial Intelligence (AI), Machine Learning (ML), and Data Science has become instrumental in driving innovation and transforming digital advertising strategies. This chapter explores the fundamentals of AI, ML, and Data Science in AdTech, examining their roles in targeting, personalization, insights generation, and optimization.

FUNDAMENTALS OF ARTIFICIAL INTELLIGENCE IN ADVERTISING

Artificial Intelligence (AI) has emerged as a game-changer in the realm of advertising, reshaping traditional practices and opening up new avenues for innovation and efficiency. At its core, AI enables advertisers to harness the power of intelligent decision-making processes and automate tasks that were once manual and time-consuming. In the dynamic landscape of AdTech, AI algorithms serve as the backbone of data analysis, uncovering intricate patterns, trends, and insights about consumer behavior, preferences, and intent.

In the context of advertising, AI-driven techniques such as Natural Language Processing (NLP), Sentiment Analysis, and Image Recognition have revolutionized the way advertisers understand and engage with their target audiences. Let's delve deeper into these fundamental aspects of AI in advertising:

1. Natural Language Processing (NLP):
NLP is a branch of AI that focuses on understanding and interpreting human language. In the context of advertising,

NLP algorithms analyze textual data from various sources, including social media posts, customer reviews, and online forums, to extract valuable insights about consumer sentiment, preferences, and intent. By processing and interpreting vast amounts of textual data, advertisers can gain a deeper understanding of consumer behavior and sentiment, enabling them to tailor their ad content and messaging to resonate with their target audience.

2. Sentiment Analysis:

Sentiment analysis, also known as opinion mining, is a technique used to determine the sentiment or emotional tone expressed in textual data. In advertising, sentiment analysis algorithms analyze customer feedback, reviews, and social media conversations to gauge consumer sentiment toward a brand, product, or campaign. By identifying positive, negative, or neutral sentiments, advertisers can gauge the effectiveness of their ad campaigns, identify areas for improvement, and adjust their messaging accordingly to enhance consumer engagement and satisfaction.

3. Image Recognition:

Image recognition technology, powered by AI, allows advertisers to analyze and interpret visual content, including images and videos, to gain insights into consumer preferences and behavior. In the realm of advertising, image recognition algorithms can identify objects, scenes, and emotions depicted in visual content, providing advertisers with valuable insights into consumer preferences and trends. By analyzing visual content shared on social media platforms, websites, and other online channels, advertisers can tailor their ad creatives and visual assets to resonate with their target audience, driving higher engagement and conversion rates.

The fundamentals of Artificial Intelligence in advertising represent a paradigm shift in the way advertisers understand

and engage with their target audiences. By leveraging AI-driven techniques such as Natural Language Processing, Sentiment Analysis, and Image Recognition, advertisers can gain valuable insights into consumer behavior and preferences, allowing them to create more personalized and targeted ad experiences that resonate with their audience on a deeper level.

LEVERAGING MACHINE LEARNING FOR TARGETING & PERSONALIZATION

Machine Learning (ML) stands as a cornerstone in the arsenal of tools available to advertisers, offering unprecedented capabilities for targeting and personalization in the realm of digital advertising. By harnessing ML algorithms, advertisers can unlock the power of data-driven insights to deliver highly targeted and personalized ad experiences that resonate with individual users on a profound level. Let's explore in detail how ML enables advertisers to optimize targeting and personalize ad campaigns:

1. Analyzing Historical Data:
At the core of ML-driven targeting and personalization lies the analysis of vast amounts of historical data. ML algorithms sift through extensive datasets containing information about user demographics, browsing behavior, purchase history, and engagement metrics to identify patterns and trends. By analyzing this wealth of data, advertisers can gain valuable insights into audience preferences, interests, and intent, laying the groundwork for more effective ad targeting and personalization strategies.

2. Identifying Relevant Audience Segments:
ML algorithms excel at segmenting audiences based on their unique characteristics and preferences. Through techniques such as clustering analysis and collaborative filtering, advertisers can identify distinct audience segments with shared interests, behaviors, and traits. By segmenting

audiences effectively, advertisers can tailor their ad campaigns to resonate with specific audience segments, delivering targeted messages and offers that are highly relevant and compelling to each group.

3. Predicting User Behavior:
ML models can predict user behavior with remarkable accuracy, enabling advertisers to anticipate user actions and preferences before they occur. By analyzing historical data and applying predictive modeling techniques, ML algorithms can forecast user engagement, conversion likelihood, and purchase intent, allowing advertisers to tailor their ad delivery strategies accordingly. By serving ads at the right time and on the right channels, advertisers can maximize the impact of their campaigns and drive higher engagement and conversion rates.

4. Optimizing Ad Delivery Strategies:
ML algorithms continuously learn and adapt to changing market dynamics, optimizing ad delivery strategies in real time to maximize performance and ROI. Through techniques such as reinforcement learning and automated bidding algorithms, advertisers can optimize ad placements, bid amounts, and targeting parameters to achieve their desired outcomes. By leveraging ML-powered optimization techniques, advertisers can allocate ad spending more effectively, minimize wastage, and achieve better results from their campaigns.

Leveraging Machine Learning for targeting and personalization empowers advertisers to deliver more relevant, engaging, and personalized ad experiences to their target audiences. By analyzing historical data, identifying relevant audience segments, predicting user behavior, and optimizing ad delivery strategies, advertisers can unlock the full potential of ML to drive better outcomes and achieve their advertising objectives with precision and efficiency.

HARNESSING DATA SCIENCE FOR INSIGHTS & OPTIMIZATION

In the dynamic landscape of digital advertising, Harnessing Data Science for Insights and Optimization represents a crucial pillar for advertisers aiming to drive impactful and efficient ad campaigns. Data Science techniques serve as the backbone of strategic decision-making processes, enabling advertisers to glean actionable insights from vast troves of data and optimize their campaigns for maximum effectiveness. Let's delve into the intricacies of how Data Science is leveraged to unlock insights and drive optimization in ad campaigns:

1. Analyzing Large Datasets:
At the heart of Data Science in advertising lies the analysis of large and complex datasets. Data scientists sift through massive volumes of data, encompassing user interactions, engagement metrics, conversion events, and more, to uncover meaningful patterns and trends. Through advanced analytical techniques such as descriptive and inferential statistics, data scientists identify correlations, anomalies, and opportunities buried within the data, laying the foundation for strategic insights and optimization strategies.

2. Extracting Actionable Insights:
Data Science empowers advertisers to extract actionable insights from the sea of data at their disposal. By applying statistical analysis, predictive modeling, and machine learning algorithms, data scientists uncover valuable insights about audience behavior, preferences, and intent. These insights inform strategic decision-making processes, guiding advertisers in identifying high-value audience segments, optimizing ad creatives and messaging, and refining targeting strategies to enhance campaign performance and ROI.

3. Predictive Modeling and Optimization:

Data Science enables advertisers to forecast future outcomes and optimize their ad campaigns through predictive modeling techniques. By building predictive models based on historical data, data scientists can anticipate user behavior, predict conversion likelihood, and forecast campaign performance metrics such as click-through rates and conversion rates. Armed with these predictive insights, advertisers can make informed decisions about budget allocation, ad placements, and targeting parameters, optimizing their campaigns for maximum impact and efficiency.

4. Experimentation and A/B Testing:

Data Science facilitates experimentation and A/B testing methodologies, allowing advertisers to test hypotheses, measure the effectiveness of different ad creatives and messaging variants, and optimize campaign performance iteratively. By designing controlled experiments and analyzing the results using statistical techniques, data scientists help advertisers identify winning strategies, refine targeting parameters, and iterate on ad creatives to continuously improve campaign performance and achieve better results over time.

Harnessing Data Science for Insights and Optimization empowers advertisers to unlock the full potential of their ad campaigns by leveraging data-driven insights and optimization strategies. By analyzing large datasets, extracting actionable insights, leveraging predictive modeling techniques, and conducting experimentation and A/B testing, advertisers can drive better outcomes, enhance campaign performance, and maximize ROI in the ever-evolving landscape of digital advertising.

CASE STUDIES

Applications of AI, ML, and Data Science in AdTech

Real-world case studies offer invaluable insights into the practical applications of Artificial Intelligence (AI), Machine Learning (ML), and Data Science in AdTech, demonstrating how these technologies drive tangible business outcomes and revolutionize advertising practices. Let's explore some compelling case studies that showcase the successful integration of AI, ML, and Data Science in AdTech:

1. Personalized Recommendations at Scale:
Case Study: Netflix
Netflix, the renowned streaming platform, has set a benchmark in delivering personalized content recommendations at an unprecedented scale. This case study delves into how Netflix utilizes advanced Artificial Intelligence (AI) and Machine Learning (ML) algorithms to provide tailored content suggestions to millions of subscribers globally, revolutionizing the streaming experience.

1. Understanding User Behavior:
Netflix's recommendation engine is powered by AI and ML algorithms that analyze vast amounts of user data, including viewing history, preferences, ratings, and interactions with the platform. By comprehensively understanding each user's behavior and preferences, Netflix can tailor its content recommendations to suit individual tastes and interests.

2. Predictive Modeling for Content Suggestions:
Netflix employs predictive modeling techniques to anticipate what content a user is likely to enjoy based on their past behavior and viewing patterns. This involves using sophisticated ML algorithms, such as collaborative filtering and content-based filtering, to identify similar users and recommend content that aligns with their interests.

3. Personalized Content Curation:

Netflix's recommendation engine curates personalized content suggestions for each user, presenting a mix of popular titles, niche genres, and new releases tailored to their preferences. By leveraging ML algorithms to continuously learn and adapt to user feedback, Netflix ensures that its recommendations remain relevant and engaging over time.

4. Continuous Improvement:

Netflix continuously refines its recommendation algorithms through iterative learning and experimentation. By analyzing user feedback, engagement metrics, and viewing trends, Netflix identifies opportunities to enhance its recommendation engine's accuracy and relevance, driving ongoing improvements in user satisfaction and retention.

5. Impact on User Engagement and Subscription Rates:

The personalized approach to content recommendation has had a significant impact on Netflix's success, driving higher levels of user engagement and increasing subscription rates. By providing users with relevant and engaging content suggestions, Netflix enhances the overall streaming experience, leading to longer viewing sessions, increased customer loyalty, and ultimately, higher subscription renewals.

6. Scalability and Global Reach:

One of the key strengths of Netflix's recommendation system is its scalability, allowing it to cater to millions of subscribers worldwide. Regardless of geographical location or cultural preferences, Netflix's AI-powered recommendations adapt to individual user preferences, demonstrating the platform's ability to deliver personalized experiences at a global scale.

7. Future Outlook:

As Netflix continues to innovate and evolve its recommendation algorithms, the platform remains at the forefront of personalized content delivery in the streaming industry. With advancements in AI and ML technology, Netflix aims to further enhance the accuracy and granularity of its recommendations, ensuring that each user receives content suggestions that resonate with their unique tastes and preferences.

In conclusion, Netflix's personalized recommendation engine exemplifies the transformative impact of AI and ML in delivering tailored content experiences to a global audience. By leveraging data-driven insights and predictive modeling, Netflix has redefined the streaming landscape, setting a high standard for personalized content delivery in the digital era.

2. Dynamic Ad Targeting:
Case Study: Amazon Advertising

Amazon Advertising, a powerhouse in the digital advertising space, employs cutting-edge Artificial Intelligence (AI) and Machine Learning (ML) algorithms to revolutionize dynamic ad targeting on its platform. This case study explores how Amazon leverages advanced technology to deliver personalized and highly effective ad experiences to users, driving conversions and maximizing return on investment (ROI) for advertisers.

1. Harnessing User Data:
At the core of Amazon's dynamic ad targeting strategy lies its vast trove of user data. Through comprehensive analysis of user browsing history, purchase behavior, product interactions, and demographic information, Amazon gains deep insights into individual user preferences and intent. This rich data ecosystem serves as the foundation for Amazon's AI-driven ad-targeting capabilities.

2. Real-Time Personalization:

Amazon's ad platform utilizes AI and ML algorithms to dynamically tailor ad content and targeting parameters in real-time. As users navigate through the Amazon ecosystem, the platform continuously analyzes their behavior and preferences to deliver relevant and personalized ad experiences. Whether it's displaying product recommendations based on past purchases or serving targeted promotions aligned with user interests, Amazon ensures that each ad is finely tuned to resonate with the individual user.

3. Precision Targeting:
Amazon's dynamic ad targeting goes beyond basic demographics to encompass a wide range of factors, including browsing history, search queries, and even contextual signals such as time of day and device type. This granular approach to targeting allows advertisers to reach highly specific audience segments with tailored messaging, increasing the likelihood of engagement and conversion.

4. Optimization through Machine Learning:
Amazon's ad platform leverages machine learning algorithms to continuously optimize ad campaigns based on performance metrics such as click-through rates (CTR), conversion rates, and return on ad spend (ROAS). By analyzing vast amounts of data and iteratively refining targeting parameters, Amazon maximizes the effectiveness of ad campaigns, driving better outcomes for advertisers while enhancing the user experience.

5. Effectiveness and ROI:
The dynamic ad targeting capabilities offered by Amazon Advertising have proven highly effective in driving conversions and maximizing ROI for advertisers. By delivering personalized ad experiences that align closely with user interests and intent, Amazon helps advertisers achieve their

marketing objectives more efficiently, resulting in higher conversion rates and improved campaign performance.

6. Compliance and Privacy:
While Amazon prioritizes personalized ad targeting, it also places a strong emphasis on user privacy and data protection. The platform adheres to strict privacy regulations and industry best practices, ensuring that user data is handled responsibly and transparently. Amazon provides users with robust privacy controls and options to manage their ad preferences, maintaining trust and confidence in its advertising ecosystem.

7. Continuous Innovation:
As technology and consumer behavior evolve, Amazon continues to innovate and enhance its dynamic ad targeting capabilities. Through ongoing investment in AI research and development, Amazon aims to stay ahead of the curve, delivering cutting-edge advertising solutions that meet the evolving needs of advertisers and users alike.

In conclusion, Amazon Advertising's dynamic ad targeting exemplifies the power of AI and ML in delivering personalized and effective advertising experiences at scale. By harnessing the vast wealth of user data and leveraging advanced algorithms, Amazon sets the standard for dynamic ad targeting in the AdTech industry, driving superior results for advertisers while delivering value to users.

3. Predictive Customer Segmentation:
Case Study: Spotify
Spotify, a dominant player in the music streaming industry, exemplifies the power of predictive customer segmentation through its innovative use of Data Science techniques. This case study delves into how Spotify leverages user data to segment its audience and personalize music

recommendations, enhancing user engagement and satisfaction on its platform.

1. Understanding User Behavior:
At the heart of Spotify's predictive customer segmentation strategy lies a deep understanding of user behavior. Spotify analyzes vast amounts of user data, including listening habits, genre preferences, playlist creations, and mood indicators, to gain insights into individual user preferences and music consumption patterns.

2. Data-Driven Segmentation:
Spotify's Data Science team employs sophisticated algorithms to segment its user base into distinct groups based on shared characteristics and behaviors. These segmentation criteria may include music genre preferences, frequency of use, device usage patterns, geographic location, and even mood indicators derived from song selections.

3. Personalized Recommendations:
Armed with insights from predictive customer segmentation, Spotify's recommendation engine delivers personalized music recommendations and curated playlists to each user. By understanding the unique tastes and preferences of different customer segments, Spotify ensures that its recommendations resonate with individual users, driving higher levels of engagement and satisfaction.

4. Dynamic Playlist Curation:
Spotify's recommendation engine dynamically curates playlists and music suggestions based on real-time user interactions and feedback. As users listen to music, skip tracks, or create playlists, Spotify's algorithms continuously adapt and refine recommendations to reflect evolving user preferences, ensuring a personalized and engaging music discovery experience.

5. Enhanced User Engagement and Retention:
The predictive customer segmentation approach employed by Spotify enhances user engagement and retention on its platform. By delivering personalized music recommendations that align closely with user preferences, Spotify encourages longer listening sessions and increased interaction with its platform, leading to higher levels of user satisfaction and loyalty over time.

6. Continuous Improvement:
Spotify's Data Science team continually iterates and improves its segmentation algorithms based on user feedback and performance metrics. By analyzing user engagement data and monitoring the effectiveness of its recommendations, Spotify identifies opportunities to refine its segmentation approach and deliver even more personalized music experiences to its users.

7. Future Outlook:
As Spotify continues to innovate and expand its platform, predictive customer segmentation will remain a cornerstone of its strategy for enhancing user engagement and satisfaction. By leveraging advanced Data Science techniques and machine learning algorithms, Spotify aims to further personalize the music discovery journey for its users, solidifying its position as a leader in the music streaming industry.

In conclusion, Spotify's predictive customer segmentation approach demonstrates the transformative impact of Data Science in delivering personalized experiences at scale. By segmenting its user base and tailoring music recommendations to individual preferences, Spotify fosters deeper connections with its users, driving higher levels of engagement, satisfaction, and loyalty on its platform.

4. Automated Ad Creative Optimization:
Case Study: Facebook Ads

Facebook Ads stands as a prime example of how Artificial Intelligence (AI) and Machine Learning (ML) revolutionize ad creative optimization through automation. This case study illuminates how Facebook employs advanced algorithms to dynamically optimize ad creatives, leveraging user engagement metrics and performance data to drive superior campaign results.

1. Harnessing User Engagement Metrics:
At the core of Facebook's ad creative optimization strategy lies a comprehensive analysis of user engagement metrics. The platform continuously monitors user interactions with ad content, including click-through rates (CTR), conversion rates, engagement levels, and other performance indicators, to glean insights into ad effectiveness and user preferences.

2. Automated A/B Testing:
Facebook's ad platform conducts automated A/B testing, where multiple ad variations are simultaneously deployed to target audiences. Through rigorous experimentation and statistical analysis, Facebook identifies which ad variations perform best in terms of user engagement and conversion metrics, allowing advertisers to optimize their creative strategies based on empirical evidence.

3. Dynamic Creative Optimization:
Facebook employs sophisticated ML algorithms to dynamically optimize ad creatives in real time. These algorithms analyze performance data and user feedback to identify high-performing ad elements, such as headlines, images, ad copy, and call-to-action buttons. By dynamically adjusting these elements based on user engagement metrics, Facebook maximizes ad relevance and effectiveness, leading to better campaign outcomes.

4. Budget Allocation Based on Performance:

Facebook's ad platform intelligently allocates the budget towards ad variations that demonstrate the highest levels of engagement and conversion rates. Through automated optimization algorithms, Facebook ensures that advertisers' budget is directed towards the most effective ad creatives, maximizing return on ad spend (ROAS) and driving better campaign results.

5. Efficiency and Resource Optimization:

The automated ad creative optimization approach employed by Facebook streamlines the campaign management process, minimizing the need for manual intervention and resources. Advertisers can leverage Facebook's AI-driven optimization capabilities to achieve better results with less effort, freeing up time and resources to focus on other strategic initiatives.

6. Continuous Improvement and Learning:

Facebook's ad platform continuously learns and adapts based on campaign performance data and user feedback. By analyzing trends and patterns in ad performance, Facebook identifies opportunities for further optimization and refinement, driving continuous improvement in ad creative strategies over time.

7. Impact on Advertiser Success:

The automated ad creative optimization capabilities offered by Facebook Ads have a significant impact on advertiser success. By delivering more relevant and engaging ad experiences to users, Facebook helps advertisers achieve their campaign objectives more effectively, whether it's increasing brand awareness, driving website traffic, or generating conversions.

8. Future Outlook:

As AI and ML technology continue to evolve, Facebook remains committed to advancing its ad creative optimization capabilities. Through ongoing innovation and investment in AI research and development, Facebook aims to further enhance its platform's ability to deliver personalized and effective ad experiences, empowering advertisers to achieve their marketing goals with greater efficiency and effectiveness.

In conclusion, Facebook Ads' automated ad creative optimization showcases the transformative potential of AI and ML in driving superior campaign results. By leveraging advanced algorithms to dynamically optimize ad creatives based on user engagement metrics and performance data, Facebook empowers advertisers to achieve better results with their ad campaigns, ultimately driving business success in the digital advertising landscape.

These case studies exemplify the successful applications of AI, ML, and Data Science in AdTech, demonstrating how these technologies drive targeted advertising, personalized recommendations, predictive segmentation, and automated optimization at scale. By adopting innovative solutions and best practices from these case studies, advertisers can harness the power of AI, ML, and Data Science to enhance their advertising strategies, drive better outcomes, and stay ahead of the competition in the ever-evolving landscape of digital advertising.

Understanding the fundamentals of AI, ML, and Data Science is essential for advertisers looking to harness the power of these technologies to enhance targeting, personalization, insights generation, and optimization in AdTech. By leveraging AI-driven techniques and data-driven approaches, advertisers can unlock new opportunities for innovation and drive better outcomes in their digital advertising efforts.

3. THE ROLE OF PRODUCT MANAGERS IN ADTECH PLATFORMS

Product Managers play a pivotal role in the dynamic and rapidly evolving landscape of Advertising Technology (AdTech) platforms. As the bridge between business objectives, user needs, and technological capabilities, Product Managers serve as the linchpin in driving the development, enhancement, and optimization of AdTech platforms. This chapter explores in detail the multifaceted role of Product Managers in AdTech platforms, highlighting their responsibilities, challenges, and key strategies for success.

STRATEGIC VISION & ROADMAPPING

In the fast-paced and dynamic realm of Advertising Technology (AdTech), Product Managers play a pivotal role in defining the strategic vision and roadmap for AdTech platforms. This involves a multifaceted approach that integrates insights from various stakeholders and market dynamics to chart a course for long-term success. Let's delve deeper into the key components of strategic vision and road mapping for Product Managers in AdTech platforms:

1. Stakeholder Collaboration:
Product Managers in AdTech platforms engage in extensive collaboration with stakeholders across the organization. This includes business leaders, engineering teams, sales and marketing professionals, and customer support representatives. By fostering open lines of communication and soliciting input from diverse perspectives, Product Managers gain a comprehensive understanding of market needs, competitive dynamics, and internal capabilities. This collaborative approach ensures that the strategic vision and

roadmap are informed by a holistic view of the business landscape.

2. Market Analysis and Trend Identification:
A crucial aspect of strategic vision and roadmapping is the analysis of market trends and technological advancements. Product Managers conduct thorough market research, monitoring industry trends, competitor activities, and emerging technologies. By staying abreast of developments in the AdTech ecosystem, Product Managers can anticipate shifts in customer preferences, regulatory changes, and technological disruptions. This foresight enables them to proactively incorporate relevant trends and innovations into the strategic roadmap, positioning the AdTech platform for sustained growth and competitiveness.

3. Alignment with Business Objectives:
Strategic vision and roadmapping must be closely aligned with overarching business objectives and goals. Product Managers work closely with executive leadership and business stakeholders to understand organizational priorities, revenue targets, and growth aspirations. By aligning the strategic roadmap with these business imperatives, Product Managers ensure that product development efforts are focused on initiatives that deliver maximum value and impact to the organization. This alignment fosters a cohesive and unified approach toward achieving strategic objectives and driving business success.

4. Innovation and Differentiation:
In the highly competitive landscape of AdTech, innovation is key to maintaining a competitive edge and driving growth. Product Managers play a critical role in driving innovation by identifying opportunities for differentiation and value creation. This may involve exploring new market segments, introducing disruptive technologies, or enhancing existing product offerings. By fostering a culture of innovation and

experimentation within the organization, Product Managers inspire creativity and drive continuous improvement, ensuring that the AdTech platform remains at the forefront of industry trends and customer expectations.

5. Long-Term Planning and Adaptability:
Strategic vision and roadmapping in AdTech require a balance between long-term planning and adaptability to changing market conditions. Product Managers develop a strategic roadmap that outlines initiatives and milestones over the coming months and years. However, they also recognize the importance of flexibility and agility in responding to unforeseen challenges and opportunities. This adaptive approach enables Product Managers to pivot quickly in response to market dynamics, regulatory changes, or shifts in customer preferences, ensuring that the AdTech platform remains agile and resilient in the face of uncertainty.

In summary, strategic vision and roadmapping are essential responsibilities for Product Managers in AdTech platforms, encompassing stakeholder collaboration, market analysis, alignment with business objectives, innovation, and adaptability. By developing a clear and comprehensive strategic roadmap, Product Managers chart a course for long-term success, driving innovation, growth, and competitive differentiation in the dynamic landscape of AdTech.

STAKEHOLDER ENGAGEMENT AND ALIGNMENT

In the intricate ecosystem of Advertising Technology (AdTech), effective stakeholder engagement and alignment are paramount for the success of Product Managers. This multifaceted responsibility entails cultivating relationships, fostering collaboration, and ensuring that all stakeholders are aligned toward common goals and objectives. Let's delve into the nuances of stakeholder engagement and alignment for Product Managers in AdTech platforms:

1. Cross-Functional Collaboration:
Product Managers serve as conduits for collaboration across diverse cross-functional teams within the organization. This includes engineering, design, marketing, sales, customer support, and other departments. By facilitating regular meetings, workshops, and brainstorming sessions, Product Managers foster a culture of collaboration and shared ownership of product development initiatives. This cross-functional collaboration ensures that all stakeholders have a voice in the decision-making process and are aligned toward achieving collective objectives.

2. Stakeholder Mapping and Communication:
Effective stakeholder engagement begins with a thorough understanding of the various stakeholders involved in the product development process. Product Managers conduct stakeholder mapping exercises to identify key stakeholders, their roles, interests, and influence levels. Armed with this knowledge, Product Managers tailor their communication strategies to engage stakeholders effectively. This may involve regular status updates, stakeholder meetings, presentations, and one-on-one discussions to keep stakeholders informed and engaged throughout the product lifecycle.

3. Soliciting Feedback and Requirements Gathering:
Product Managers actively solicit feedback from stakeholders to gather insights, validate assumptions, and gather requirements for product enhancements. This feedback may come from internal stakeholders, such as engineering teams providing technical insights, or external stakeholders, such as customers providing user feedback. By actively listening to stakeholder feedback and incorporating it into the product development process, Product Managers ensure that products are aligned with customer needs, preferences, and expectations.

4. Advocating for Stakeholder Needs:
Product Managers act as advocates for stakeholder needs, representing the interests of both internal and external stakeholders throughout the product development lifecycle. This involves advocating for resources, prioritizing features based on stakeholder requirements, and addressing any concerns or challenges that arise. By championing stakeholder needs, Product Managers ensure that product development efforts are aligned with business priorities and customer requirements, ultimately driving customer satisfaction and business success.

5. Conflict Resolution and Consensus Building:
In the dynamic and fast-paced environment of AdTech, conflicts and disagreements among stakeholders are inevitable. Product Managers play a crucial role in mediating conflicts, facilitating constructive dialogue, and building consensus among stakeholders with competing interests. This may involve negotiating trade-offs, finding common ground, and aligning stakeholders toward mutually beneficial outcomes. By fostering a collaborative and inclusive environment, Product Managers mitigate conflicts and ensure that all stakeholders are aligned toward achieving shared goals.

Effective stakeholder engagement and alignment are essential responsibilities for Product Managers in AdTech platforms, encompassing cross-functional collaboration, stakeholder mapping, communication, feedback solicitation, advocacy, conflict resolution, and consensus building. By fostering strong relationships, advocating for stakeholder needs, and driving alignment across diverse teams, Product Managers ensure that product development efforts are aligned with business priorities and customer requirements, driving success and innovation in the dynamic landscape of AdTech.

PRODUCT DEVELOPMENT AND EXECUTION

In the fast-paced and dynamic world of Advertising Technology (AdTech), Product Managers play a central role in orchestrating the end-to-end product development lifecycle. This multifaceted responsibility encompasses a wide array of tasks and activities aimed at translating market needs into tangible product features and functionalities. Let's explore the intricacies of product development and execution for Product Managers in AdTech platforms:

1. Concept Ideation and Requirements Gathering:
Product Managers kickstart the product development process by collaborating with stakeholders to define product requirements and specifications. This involves conducting market research, gathering user feedback, and analyzing industry trends to identify opportunities for innovation and differentiation. By synthesizing insights from various sources, Product Managers develop a clear understanding of customer needs, pain points, and preferences, laying the groundwork for product ideation and conceptualization.

2. Roadmap Planning and Prioritization:
Once product requirements are defined, Product Managers create a strategic roadmap that outlines key initiatives and milestones for the product's development. This roadmap serves as a guiding framework for prioritizing features, setting timelines, and allocating resources effectively. Product Managers collaborate with cross-functional teams, including engineering, design, and marketing, to prioritize development efforts based on business impact, technical feasibility, and user feedback. By balancing competing priorities and trade-offs, Product Managers ensure that the product roadmap aligns with business objectives and customer needs.

3. Collaboration with Engineering Teams:
Product Managers work closely with engineering teams throughout the product development lifecycle to bring the product vision to life. They collaborate with software engineers, data scientists, and other technical experts to translate market requirements into actionable development tasks and user stories. Product Managers provide guidance, clarification, and support to engineering teams, ensuring that product features are implemented according to specifications, within budget, and on schedule. Through effective communication and collaboration, Product Managers foster a culture of teamwork and accountability, driving the successful execution of product initiatives.

4. Agile Project Management and Iterative Development:
Agile methodologies such as Scrum and Kanban are commonly employed in AdTech product development to facilitate iterative and incremental delivery. Product Managers leverage Agile principles to break down complex projects into manageable tasks, prioritize work based on business value, and adapt to changing requirements and priorities. They lead Agile ceremonies such as sprint planning, daily stand-ups, and retrospectives, providing direction and guidance to cross-functional teams. By embracing Agile project management practices, Product Managers foster a culture of adaptability, transparency, and continuous improvement, driving efficient and effective product development.

5. Quality Assurance and Testing:
Ensuring product quality and reliability is a top priority for Product Managers in AdTech platforms. They collaborate with quality assurance (QA) teams to define testing strategies, develop test plans, and execute comprehensive testing protocols to validate product functionality and performance. Product Managers oversee the testing process, analyze test results, and prioritize bug fixes and enhancements based on

severity and impact. By maintaining rigorous quality standards and conducting thorough testing, Product Managers ensure that the final product meets user expectations and delivers a seamless user experience.

6. Launch and Post-launch Monitoring:
Product Managers oversee the product launch process, coordinating cross-functional efforts to ensure a successful rollout. They collaborate with marketing, sales, and customer support teams to develop go-to-market strategies, create marketing collateral, and train internal stakeholders. Following the product launch, Product Managers monitor key performance indicators (KPIs), gather user feedback, and iterate on the product based on user insights and market feedback. By continuously monitoring product performance and iterating based on user feedback, Product Managers drive ongoing improvement and innovation, ensuring that the product remains competitive and aligned with evolving market needs.

Product Managers play a critical role in overseeing the end-to-end product development lifecycle in AdTech platforms, from concept ideation to launch and beyond. Through effective collaboration, strategic planning, agile project management, and relentless focus on quality and user satisfaction, Product Managers drive the successful execution of product initiatives, delivering innovative solutions that meet customer needs and drive business growth in the dynamic landscape of AdTech.

USER-CENTRIC DESIGN & EXPERIENCE

In the realm of Advertising Technology (AdTech), user experience (UX) plays a pivotal role in shaping the success of products and platforms. Product Managers in AdTech platforms prioritize user-centric design and experience as a core aspect of their responsibilities. Let's explore in detail how Product Managers ensure that user experience remains at the forefront of product development in AdTech:

1. Collaborating with Design Teams:
Product Managers work closely with design teams to translate user needs and requirements into intuitive and visually appealing user interfaces. They collaborate with user experience (UX) designers, graphic designers, and interaction designers to create wireframes, mockups, and prototypes that embody the desired user experience. Product Managers provide input, feedback, and direction to design teams, ensuring that design decisions align with user needs, platform capabilities, and industry best practices.

2. Conducting User Research:
Understanding user needs, preferences, and pain points is fundamental to delivering a user-centric product experience. Product Managers conduct user research activities such as surveys, interviews, focus groups, and usability testing to gather qualitative and quantitative insights into user behavior and preferences. They analyze user feedback, observe user interactions, and identify patterns and trends that inform design decisions and product enhancements. By incorporating user research findings into the product development process, Product Managers ensure that products are tailored to meet the needs and expectations of their target audience.

3. Iterative Design and Prototyping:
Product Managers advocate for an iterative approach to design and prototyping, allowing for continuous refinement and improvement based on user feedback and testing results. They collaborate with design teams to create prototypes and interactive mockups that can be tested with real users to validate design assumptions and identify areas for improvement. Product Managers facilitate usability testing

sessions, gather feedback from participants, and iterate on design iterations to address usability issues, optimize user flows, and enhance overall user experience.

4. Analyzing User Behavior Data:
Data-driven insights play a crucial role in informing design decisions and optimizing user experience in AdTech platforms. Product Managers leverage analytics tools and user behavior data to gain insights into how users interact with the platform, identify pain points, and uncover opportunities for improvement. They analyze metrics such as user engagement, click-through rates, bounce rates, and conversion rates to assess the effectiveness of design changes and inform future iterations. By using data to drive decision-making, Product Managers ensure that design enhancements are grounded in empirical evidence and aligned with user needs and preferences.

5. Championing User-Centric Culture:
Product Managers foster a culture of user-centricity within the organization, advocating for the prioritization of user experience across all stages of product development. They educate cross-functional teams about the importance of UX design principles, usability best practices, and the value of user feedback. Product Managers encourage collaboration between product, design, engineering, and marketing teams to ensure that user experience considerations are integrated into every aspect of the product development process. By championing a user-centric culture, Product Managers empower teams to deliver products that delight users and drive business success.

User-Centric Design and Experience are core pillars of product development in AdTech platforms, with Product Managers playing a central role in ensuring that user needs, preferences, and expectations are prioritized throughout the product development lifecycle. By collaborating with design teams, conducting user research, iterating on design prototypes, analyzing user behavior data, and championing a user-centric culture, Product Managers drive the creation of products that deliver intuitive, engaging, and satisfying user experiences, ultimately driving customer satisfaction, retention, and loyalty on the AdTech platform.

PERFORMANCE MONITORING AND OPTIMIZATION

In the dynamic and competitive landscape of Advertising Technology (AdTech), Product Managers bear the responsibility of continuously monitoring the performance of their products and optimizing them for sustained success and growth. Performance monitoring and optimization are critical aspects of a Product Manager's role, ensuring that products remain effective, efficient, and aligned with business objectives. Let's explore in detail how Product Managers oversee performance monitoring and optimization in AdTech platforms:

1. Defining Key Performance Indicators (KPIs):
Product Managers collaborate with stakeholders to define key performance indicators (KPIs) that align with business objectives and strategic goals. These KPIs may include metrics such as user engagement, conversion rates, retention rates, revenue growth, and customer satisfaction. By establishing clear and measurable KPIs, Product Managers set benchmarks for evaluating the performance of their products and tracking progress over time.

2. Monitoring Product Performance:
Product Managers utilize analytics tools and data dashboards to monitor the performance of their products in real time. They track KPIs, analyze user behavior data, and identify trends and patterns that provide insights into product performance and user satisfaction. By continuously

monitoring product performance, Product Managers gain visibility into how users interact with the product, identify areas of strength and weakness, and uncover opportunities for improvement.

3. Identifying Optimization Opportunities:
Based on insights gathered from performance monitoring activities, Product Managers identify opportunities for optimization and enhancement. This may involve analyzing user feedback, conducting usability studies, and benchmarking against industry standards and best practices. Product Managers prioritize optimization opportunities based on their potential impact on key business metrics and the resources required for implementation.

4. Iterative Improvement through Experimentation:
Product Managers leverage data-driven experimentation techniques such as A/B testing, multivariate testing, and user segmentation to iteratively improve product performance and user experience. They develop hypotheses, design experiments, and measure the impact of changes on key metrics to validate assumptions and inform decision-making. By conducting controlled experiments, Product Managers mitigate risks associated with product changes and ensure that optimizations deliver tangible benefits to users and the business.

5. Collaboration with Cross-Functional Teams:
Performance monitoring and optimization efforts require close collaboration with cross-functional teams, including engineering, design, marketing, and analytics. Product Managers work collaboratively to prioritize optimization initiatives, allocate resources effectively, and coordinate implementation efforts. They foster a culture of experimentation, data-driven decision-making, and continuous improvement across the organization,

empowering teams to innovate and optimize products iteratively.

6. Continuous Learning and Adaptation:
In the rapidly evolving landscape of AdTech, Product Managers embrace a mindset of continuous learning and adaptation. They stay abreast of industry trends, emerging technologies, and best practices in performance monitoring and optimization. Product Managers seek opportunities to experiment with new approaches, tools, and methodologies, learning from successes and failures to refine their optimization strategies over time.

Performance Monitoring and Optimization are essential components of a Product Manager's role in AdTech platforms, ensuring that products remain effective, efficient, and aligned with business objectives. By defining key performance indicators, monitoring product performance, identifying optimization opportunities, conducting data-driven experiments, collaborating with cross-functional teams, and embracing a culture of continuous learning, Product Managers drive sustained improvement and innovation, delivering value to users and driving business growth in the competitive landscape of AdTech.

Product Managers play a multifaceted role in AdTech platforms, encompassing strategic visioning, stakeholder engagement, product development, user experience design, and performance optimization. By leveraging their cross-functional expertise, analytical skills, and customer-centric mindset, Product Managers drive the success of AdTech platforms, delivering innovative solutions that meet the evolving needs of advertisers, publishers, and users in the digital advertising ecosystem.

4. BUILDING THE BEST PRODUCTS WITH AI & ML TOOLS

In today's digital advertising landscape, the integration of artificial intelligence (AI) and machine learning (ML) into AdTech platforms has become imperative for staying competitive and delivering impactful advertising campaigns. This chapter explores the opportunities and challenges associated with incorporating AI and ML into AdTech products, strategies for implementation, and real-world case studies showcasing the transformative power of AI-driven AdTech solutions.

INCORPORATING AI & ML INTO ADTECH PLATFORMS

The integration of AI and ML into AdTech platforms has the potential to revolutionize the digital advertising industry by enabling more precise targeting, optimizing campaign performance, and delivering personalized ad experiences to users. AI algorithms can analyze vast amounts of data in real time, uncovering actionable insights and predictive patterns that drive more effective advertising strategies. This can lead to increased efficiency, productivity, and user engagement, fostering brand loyalty and ultimately, increasing conversion rates.

One of the key advantages of AI in AdTech is the ability to automate advertising campaigns. AI-based tools can help create eye-catching ads, target specific audiences, optimize bids, and track performance in a detailed way. These tools can uncover hidden patterns within the data and identify audience segments that share common characteristics or interests. For example, AI can analyze user interactions with ads, such as dwell time, scroll depth, or facial expressions, to gauge user engagement levels and sentiment toward the content. These insights can help advertisers refine their ad strategies, tailor messaging, and optimize user experiences to drive better results.

Personalization at scale is another area where AI plays a pivotal role in AdTech. Through machine learning algorithms, adtech professionals can leverage AI to analyze user behavior, preferences, and contextual data to deliver highly personalized advertisements. With the power of AI, advertisers can dynamically adjust ad elements such as images, headlines, and calls to action based on real-time user data. This level of personalization goes beyond simple demographic targeting and enables advertisers to deliver hyper-targeted ads that align with users' interests and preferences, enhancing the overall ad experience and increasing the likelihood of positive engagement.

However, incorporating AI and ML into AdTech platforms also poses challenges. Data privacy concerns are a significant issue, as the vast amount of data processed in programmatic advertising requires safeguards to protect it from breaches and unauthorized access. Ensuring data security is crucial to maintaining the integrity of AI-driven programmatic advertising. Additionally, algorithmic bias is a concern, as AI models trained on biased data can perpetuate and exacerbate existing disparities. Ensuring that AI models are fair, transparent, and accountable is essential for building trust and avoiding potential legal issues.

The need for skilled personnel to develop and maintain AI-driven solutions is another challenge. As AI continues to integrate into AdTech platforms, professionals need to be aware of the ethical considerations that come with this technology and stay abreast of emerging trends and ethical considerations. AdTech professionals who embrace AI-driven technologies can automate processes, make data-driven decisions, deliver personalized experiences, and gain valuable audience insights. By staying up-to-date with emerging AI trends and ethical considerations, professionals can position themselves as leaders in this evolving field

The integration of AI and ML into AdTech platforms presents numerous opportunities for enhancing targeting precision, optimizing campaign performance, and delivering personalized ad experiences to users. However, it also poses challenges, including data privacy concerns, algorithmic bias, and the need for skilled personnel to develop and maintain AI-driven solutions. By addressing these challenges and staying abreast of emerging trends and ethical considerations, AdTech professionals can unlock new horizons of success and shape the future of advertising.

STRATEGIES FOR IMPLEMENTING AI & ML SOLUTIONS

Implementing AI and ML solutions in AdTech products requires a strategic approach that encompasses data acquisition, algorithm selection, model training, and deployment. Product managers and developers must collaborate closely to identify use cases where AI and ML can add value, assess the feasibility of implementation, and prioritize initiatives based on their potential impact on business objectives. Additionally, investing in data infrastructure, talent acquisition, and ongoing training is essential for building AI and ML capabilities within AdTech organizations.

Data Acquisition and Preparation:
To effectively implement AI and ML solutions in AdTech, it is crucial to have access to high-quality, relevant data. Data acquisition can involve gathering user data, contextual data, and historical campaign performance data from various sources, such as ad exchanges, demand-side platforms (DSPs), and supply-side platforms (SSPs). The data must be

cleaned, preprocessed, and transformed into a format suitable for machine learning algorithms.

Algorithm Selection and Model Training:
Selecting the appropriate AI and ML algorithms is critical for successful implementation. This process involves understanding the specific use case, identifying the most suitable algorithms, and training the models using the prepared data. Common algorithms used in AdTech include decision trees, neural networks, and reinforcement learning algorithms. Model training involves adjusting the parameters of the algorithm to optimize performance and minimize errors.

Deployment and Monitoring:
Once the AI and ML models are trained, they must be integrated into the AdTech platform. This involves deploying the models into the production environment and monitoring their performance to ensure they are delivering the expected results. Ongoing monitoring is essential to identify any issues, such as model drift, and to make necessary adjustments to maintain optimal performance.

Investing in Data Infrastructure, Talent, and Training:
Building AI and ML capabilities within AdTech organizations requires significant investment in data infrastructure, talent acquisition, and ongoing training. This includes investing in data storage and processing systems, hiring data scientists and machine learning engineers, and providing ongoing training to keep up with emerging trends and technologies.

Data Privacy and Ethical Considerations:
Data privacy and ethical considerations are critical when implementing AI and ML solutions in AdTech. This involves ensuring that data is collected and used in compliance with relevant regulations, such as GDPR and CCPA, and that AI and ML models are transparent, fair, and unbiased.

Implementing AI and ML solutions in AdTech products requires a strategic approach that encompasses data acquisition, algorithm selection, model training, and deployment. By investing in data infrastructure, talent acquisition, and ongoing training, AdTech organizations can build AI and ML capabilities that deliver significant value to their customers, while also addressing data privacy and ethical considerations.

AUTOMATING COMPLEX PROCESSES WITH MICROSERVICES ARCHITECTURE

Microservices architecture stands as a pivotal framework in automating complex processes within AdTech platforms, offering scalability, flexibility, and agility. This section elaborates on how AdTech companies harness microservices to streamline development workflows, enhance system reliability, and expedite the delivery of new features and improvements.

1. Breaking Down Monolithic Applications:
Traditionally, AdTech platforms often rely on monolithic applications, where all components are tightly coupled into a single, large codebase. Microservices architecture advocates for breaking down these monolithic applications into smaller, self-contained services, each responsible for a specific business function or process. This decomposition enables greater modularity and independence, allowing teams to develop, deploy, and scale services autonomously.

2. Streamlining Development Workflows:
Microservices architecture fosters agility and innovation by streamlining development workflows. Since each microservice operates independently, development teams can work on individual services concurrently, without dependencies or conflicts. This parallel development

approach accelerates the pace of development, enabling AdTech companies to iterate rapidly and respond promptly to market demands and customer feedback.

3. Improving System Reliability:
Microservices architecture enhances system reliability by isolating failures and minimizing their impact on the overall system. In a monolithic architecture, a single component failure can potentially bring down the entire application. In contrast, microservices are resilient to failures, as faults are contained within individual services and do not propagate across the system. Additionally, microservices can be designed for scalability and fault tolerance, ensuring high availability and performance under varying workloads.

4. Accelerating Time-to-Market:
Microservices architecture accelerates time-to-market for new features and enhancements, enabling AdTech companies to stay competitive in a fast-paced industry. With microservices, developers can introduce changes to specific services without disrupting the entire application. This decoupling of services allows for faster deployment cycles, enabling AdTech platforms to deliver value to customers more efficiently and adapt to market trends swiftly.

5. Integrating AI and ML Capabilities:
Microservices architecture facilitates the integration of Artificial Intelligence (AI) and Machine Learning (ML) capabilities into AdTech platforms. AI and ML algorithms can be encapsulated within microservices, enabling AdTech companies to leverage advanced analytics, predictive modeling, and recommendation engines to enhance targeting, personalization, and campaign optimization. By embedding AI and ML capabilities into microservices, AdTech platforms can adapt and evolve in real time to meet changing market dynamics and user preferences.

In summary, microservices architecture empowers AdTech companies to automate complex processes, drive innovation, and deliver value to customers more effectively. By embracing microservices, AdTech platforms can achieve scalability, flexibility, and resilience, positioning themselves for success in a rapidly evolving digital advertising landscape.

CASE STUDIES OF AI-DRIVEN ADTECH PRODUCTS

This section showcases real-world case studies highlighting the transformative impact of AI-driven AdTech products across various use cases:

1. AI-Driven Personalized Ad Targeting: Case Study
A prominent AdTech platform exemplifies the transformative power of Artificial Intelligence (AI) in enhancing personalized ad targeting strategies. This case study elucidates how the platform leveraged AI algorithms to analyze user behavior and preferences, enabling advertisers to deliver highly targeted and relevant ads to individual users, consequently driving higher engagement rates and improved ROI on advertising spend.

Understanding User Behavior:
At the heart of the AI-driven personalized ad targeting strategy lies a comprehensive understanding of user behavior. The AdTech platform harnesses vast amounts of data, including browsing history, search queries, purchase behavior, and demographic information, to gain insights into individual user preferences and interests.

Predictive Analytics and Segmentation:
The platform employs advanced AI algorithms, including machine learning and predictive analytics, to segment audiences based on shared characteristics and behaviors. By analyzing historical data patterns and user interactions, the

platform identifies distinct audience segments with unique preferences and affinities.

Personalized Ad Delivery:
Armed with insights from predictive analytics and segmentation, advertisers can tailor their ad campaigns to specific audience segments. The platform dynamically delivers personalized ads to individual users based on their interests, browsing history, and purchase intent, ensuring relevance and resonance with the target audience.

Optimization and Performance Tracking:
The AI-driven ad targeting platform continuously optimizes ad campaigns based on real-time performance data. By monitoring key metrics such as click-through rates (CTR), conversion rates, and return on ad spend (ROAS), advertisers can gauge the effectiveness of their ads and adjust targeting parameters accordingly to maximize ROI.

Enhanced Engagement and Conversion Rates:
The personalized ad targeting approach yields tangible benefits for advertisers, including higher engagement rates and conversion rates. By delivering ads that resonate with individual users' interests and preferences, advertisers capture the attention of their target audience more effectively, resulting in increased click-throughs, conversions, and ultimately, greater ROI on advertising spend.

Data Privacy and Compliance:
The AdTech platform prioritizes data privacy and compliance throughout the ad targeting process. Advertisers adhere to stringent data protection regulations, such as GDPR and CCPA, ensuring that user data is handled responsibly and transparently, and user privacy is safeguarded at all times.

Continuous Innovation and Evolution:
The AI-driven personalized ad targeting platform is continuously evolving and innovating to stay ahead of market trends and meet advertisers' evolving needs. The platform invests in research and development to enhance its AI algorithms, improve targeting accuracy, and explore new ways to deliver personalized ad experiences to users.

Future Outlook:
As AI technology advances and consumer expectations evolve, personalized ad targeting will continue to play a central role in digital advertising strategies. The AI-driven personalized ad targeting platform remains committed to driving innovation, delivering value to advertisers, and enhancing the ad experience for users in the ever-changing digital landscape.

2. AI-Driven Predictive Campaign Optimization: Case Study
This case study delves into the transformative impact of Artificial Intelligence (AI) on campaign optimization within the AdTech industry. It outlines how an AI-driven AdTech solution harnesses machine learning models to predict campaign performance metrics, optimize ad placements, and refine bidding strategies in real time, enabling advertisers to achieve their advertising objectives more efficiently.

Leveraging Machine Learning Models:
The AI-driven AdTech solution employs advanced machine learning models to analyze vast volumes of historical campaign data, user interactions, and market trends. These models utilize sophisticated algorithms to identify patterns, correlations, and predictive signals that influence campaign performance metrics, such as click-through rates (CTR) and conversion rates.

Predictive Analytics for Campaign Performance:
By leveraging predictive analytics, the AdTech solution forecasts campaign performance metrics before the campaign launch. Predictive models factor in various parameters, including audience demographics, ad creatives, targeting criteria, and historical performance data, to generate accurate predictions of future campaign outcomes.

Real-Time Optimization Strategies:
The AI-driven AdTech solution continuously monitors campaign performance in real time, comparing actual results against predicted outcomes. Leveraging this real-time data, the solution dynamically adjusts ad placements, bidding strategies, and targeting parameters to optimize campaign performance and maximize ROI.

Maximizing Campaign Effectiveness:
Through predictive campaign optimization, advertisers can maximize campaign effectiveness by allocating resources to high-performing ad placements and targeting segments. The AI-driven solution identifies opportunities to improve ad performance, minimize wasteful spending, and enhance overall campaign efficiency, ultimately driving better results for advertisers.

Achieving Advertising Objectives Efficiently:
By harnessing AI-driven predictive campaign optimization, advertisers can achieve their advertising objectives more efficiently. Whether the goal is to increase brand awareness, drive website traffic, or generate leads and conversions, the AdTech solution enables advertisers to tailor their strategies and tactics to align with their specific objectives and desired outcomes.

Continuous Learning and Improvement:
The AI-driven AdTech solution operates on a continuous learning loop, refining its predictive models and optimization

algorithms over time. By analyzing feedback from campaign performance data and incorporating new insights, the solution evolves to adapt to changing market dynamics, emerging trends, and evolving advertiser goals.

Adapting to Market Trends:
In a rapidly evolving advertising landscape, the ability to adapt to market trends is crucial for advertisers. The AI-driven AdTech solution enables advertisers to stay ahead of the curve by leveraging predictive analytics to anticipate shifts in consumer behavior, competitor activity, and industry trends, enabling proactive adjustments to campaign strategies.

Future Outlook:
As AI technology continues to advance, predictive campaign optimization will remain a cornerstone of digital advertising strategies. The AI-driven AdTech solution remains committed to innovation, leveraging the latest advancements in machine learning and predictive analytics to empower advertisers with the tools and insights they need to succeed in an increasingly competitive marketplace.

3. AI-Driven Dynamic Creative Optimization: Case Study
This case study highlights the transformative role of Artificial Intelligence (AI) in dynamic creative optimization (DCO) within the AdTech industry. It showcases how an AdTech platform utilized AI algorithms to customize ad creatives in real-time based on user context and preferences, leading to higher engagement and conversion rates, and ultimately, improved campaign performance and brand visibility.

Understanding User Context and Preferences:
At the core of dynamic creative optimization lies a deep understanding of user context and preferences. The AdTech platform gathers extensive data on user behavior, including browsing history, demographic information, and past interactions with ads, to create comprehensive user profiles.

2. Leveraging AI Algorithms for Real-Time Customization:
The platform employs advanced AI algorithms to dynamically optimize ad creatives in real time. These algorithms analyze user profiles, contextual signals, and real-time data streams to tailor ad content, imagery, and messaging to match individual user preferences and behavior patterns.

Real-Time Adjustments and Personalization:
Through AI-driven dynamic creative optimization, ad content is automatically adjusted and personalized on the fly. For example, if a user is browsing for outdoor gear, the ad might showcase relevant products and imagery related to hiking or camping, maximizing relevance and resonance with the user.

Higher Engagement and Conversion Rates:
By delivering personalized and contextually relevant ad experiences, advertisers achieved higher engagement and conversion rates. Users were more likely to interact with ads that resonated with their interests and preferences, leading to increased click-through rates (CTR), conversions, and ultimately, improved campaign performance.

Improved Campaign Performance and Brand Visibility:
The implementation of dynamic creative optimization using AI algorithms resulted in improved campaign performance and brand visibility for advertisers. Advertisers were able to deliver more impactful and memorable ad experiences that captured the attention of their target audience, driving brand awareness and affinity.

Continuous Optimization and Learning:
The AI-driven dynamic creative optimization process operates on a continuous optimization loop. Ad performance data is constantly analyzed, and insights are fed back into the system to refine targeting, messaging, and creative elements

further. This iterative approach enables advertisers to continuously improve ad performance over time.

Adapting to User Preferences and Trends:
In a fast-paced digital landscape, the ability to adapt to changing user preferences and trends is essential. The AI-driven dynamic creative optimization platform enables advertisers to stay ahead of the curve by dynamically adjusting ad creatives to align with evolving user interests, preferences, and market trends.

Future Outlook:
As AI technology continues to evolve, dynamic creative optimization will remain a cornerstone of effective advertising strategies. The AI-driven AdTech platform remains committed to innovation, leveraging the latest advancements in AI and machine learning to empower advertisers with the tools and insights they need to create compelling, personalized ad experiences that drive results.

These case studies demonstrate the diverse applications of AI and ML in AdTech, illustrating how these technologies are revolutionizing the way advertisers target, engage, and convert audiences in today's digital advertising ecosystem.

5. DATA SCIENCE TECHNIQUES FOR COMPLEX DATA POINTS

In the dynamic landscape of digital advertising, the effective management of rich and complex data is essential for driving targeted campaigns, optimizing ad placements, and measuring campaign performance. This chapter delves into the critical role of data science in managing complex data points within AdTech platforms, covering topics such as building and maintaining data lakes, advanced analytics for extracting insights and ensuring data quality, privacy, and compliance.

THE ROLE OF DATA SCIENCE

Data science is integral to the functioning of AdTech platforms, as it enables the management and analysis of the vast amounts of data generated within the advertising ecosystem. AdTech companies deal with a diverse range of data types, including user interactions, ad impressions, demographic information, and campaign metrics. This data deluge presents both opportunities and challenges, requiring sophisticated analytical techniques to extract meaningful insights and drive informed decision-making. In this section, we delve into the pivotal role of data science in AdTech and how it empowers advertisers to optimize their advertising strategies.

1. Data Collection and Aggregation:
AdTech platforms collect data from various sources, including websites, mobile apps, and connected devices. Data scientists are responsible for aggregating and integrating this disparate data into a centralized repository for analysis. They ensure data quality and consistency by implementing data

cleaning and preprocessing techniques to remove duplicates, handle missing values, and standardize data formats.

2. Statistical Analysis:
Data scientists employ statistical analysis to explore data distributions, identify outliers, and measure central tendencies. Descriptive statistics provide insights into the characteristics of the data, such as mean, median, and variance, while inferential statistics enable hypothesis testing and confidence interval estimation. Statistical techniques such as regression analysis and hypothesis testing help assess the relationships between variables and uncover significant factors influencing ad performance.

3. Machine Learning Algorithms:
Machine learning algorithms play a pivotal role in predictive modeling, pattern recognition, and personalized ad targeting. Data scientists leverage supervised learning techniques, such as classification and regression, to build predictive models that forecast user behavior, predict ad engagement, and optimize ad placements. Unsupervised learning algorithms, such as clustering and dimensionality reduction, enable segmentation analysis and audience profiling, allowing advertisers to target specific user segments with tailored ad content.

4. Data Visualization:
Data visualization tools are essential for communicating insights and findings to stakeholders effectively. Data scientists use visualization techniques, such as charts, graphs, and dashboards, to illustrate trends, patterns, and correlations within the data. Visualization tools like Tableau, Power BI, and Matplotlib enable interactive exploration of data and facilitate data-driven decision-making by providing intuitive and informative visual representations.

5. A/B Testing and Experimentation:
Data scientists design and analyze A/B tests and experiments to evaluate the effectiveness of ad campaigns and marketing strategies. They formulate hypotheses, define experimental variables, and design test cases to measure the impact of changes on key performance metrics such as click-through rates, conversion rates, and return on investment. Through rigorous experimentation and data analysis, data scientists provide actionable insights for optimizing ad creatives, targeting parameters, and campaign settings.

6. Performance Monitoring and Optimization:
Data scientists monitor the performance of ad campaigns in real time and conduct ongoing analysis to identify optimization opportunities. They develop algorithms and models to automate bid adjustments, budget allocation, and ad targeting based on dynamic market conditions and user behavior. Continuous optimization efforts, guided by data-driven insights, enable advertisers to maximize campaign effectiveness, minimize costs, and achieve their advertising goals.

Data science plays a multifaceted role in the AdTech industry, from data collection and preprocessing to statistical analysis, machine learning, and performance optimization. By leveraging advanced analytical techniques and data-driven insights, advertisers can enhance targeting precision, improve campaign ROI, and deliver more relevant and engaging ad experiences to their target audience. As AdTech continues to evolve, the role of data science will remain indispensable in driving innovation, efficiency, and competitiveness in the digital advertising ecosystem.

BUILDING & MAINTAINING DATA LAKES

Building and maintaining data lakes is fundamental for AdTech companies to effectively manage the vast volumes of data generated within their platforms. This section explores the importance of data lakes, their role in storing and processing data, and the key considerations for building and maintaining them within the AdTech industry.

1. Importance of Data Lakes:
Data lakes serve as centralized repositories for storing raw data from various sources in its native format. They provide a scalable and cost-effective solution for managing large volumes of data, including user interactions, ad impressions, demographic information, and campaign metrics. By consolidating data in a single location, data lakes enable AdTech companies to perform comprehensive analysis and derive actionable insights to drive advertising strategies.

2. Data Ingestion:
Data lakes facilitate the ingestion of raw data from diverse sources, such as ad servers, web analytics platforms, and third-party data providers. AdTech companies utilize data ingestion tools and processes to collect data in real-time or batch mode and load it into the data lake for further processing and analysis. Data ingestion pipelines ensure that data is efficiently and securely transferred to the data lake while maintaining data quality and integrity.

3. Processing and Analysis:
Data scientists leverage distributed computing frameworks like Apache Hadoop and Apache Spark to process and analyze data stored in data lakes. These frameworks enable parallel processing of data across distributed computing nodes, allowing for efficient querying, transformation, and analysis of large datasets. Data lakes support a wide range of analytical tasks, including descriptive statistics, predictive

modeling, and machine learning algorithms, to extract insights and patterns from the data.

4. Scalability and Flexibility:
Data lakes offer scalability and flexibility to accommodate growing data volumes and diverse data types within the AdTech ecosystem. As data sources and requirements evolve, data lakes can scale horizontally by adding additional storage and computing resources to meet the growing demands for data storage and processing. Additionally, data lakes support a variety of data formats, including structured, semi-structured, and unstructured data, making them suitable for storing diverse data types generated by AdTech platforms.

5. Data Governance and Security:
Implementing robust data governance policies and security measures is crucial for maintaining data integrity, privacy, and compliance within data lakes. AdTech companies establish data governance frameworks to define data ownership, access controls, and data lifecycle management policies. They implement encryption, access controls, and auditing mechanisms to protect sensitive data and ensure compliance with regulations such as GDPR and CCPA.

6. Maintenance and Optimization:
Regular maintenance and optimization are essential for ensuring the reliability, performance, and efficiency of data lakes. AdTech companies monitor data lake usage, performance metrics, and storage utilization to identify bottlenecks and optimize resource allocation. They conduct regular data quality checks, data validation, and metadata management to ensure data consistency and accuracy within the data lake. Additionally, implementing data retention policies and data archiving strategies helps manage data lifecycle and storage costs effectively.

Building and maintaining data lakes is critical for AdTech companies to harness the power of data and derive actionable insights to drive advertising strategies. By establishing scalable and flexible data lake architectures, implementing robust data governance and security measures, and conducting regular maintenance and optimization, AdTech companies can effectively manage and analyze large volumes of data to gain a competitive edge in the digital advertising landscape.

ADVANCED ANALYTICS FOR EXTRACTING INSIGHTS

Advanced analytics techniques play a crucial role in helping AdTech companies derive actionable insights from the vast amounts of data they collect. This section explores various advanced analytics methods utilized in the AdTech industry, including predictive modeling, segmentation analysis, and anomaly detection, and how they contribute to informed decision-making.

1. Predictive Modeling:
Predictive modeling involves using historical data to make predictions about future outcomes. AdTech companies leverage predictive modeling techniques such as regression analysis, decision trees, and neural networks to forecast campaign performance metrics, such as click-through rates (CTR), conversion rates, and return on investment (ROI). By analyzing historical data on ad impressions, user interactions, and campaign metrics, advertisers can identify patterns and trends that inform predictive models. These models help advertisers optimize ad targeting strategies, allocate budgets effectively, and forecast campaign outcomes with greater accuracy.

2. Segmentation Analysis:
Segmentation analysis involves dividing a target audience into distinct groups based on shared characteristics or

behaviors. AdTech companies utilize segmentation analysis to understand their audience better and tailor their advertising strategies accordingly. By segmenting audiences based on demographics, interests, geographic location, or purchasing behavior, advertisers can create personalized ad experiences that resonate with specific audience segments. Segmentation analysis enables advertisers to target high-value audiences, optimize ad creative and messaging, and improve overall campaign performance.

3. Anomaly Detection:
Anomaly detection techniques identify outliers or irregularities in the data that deviate significantly from the expected patterns. In the context of AdTech, anomaly detection helps advertisers detect fraudulent activity, bot traffic, or other anomalous behaviors that may impact campaign performance or skew analytics metrics. AdTech companies employ anomaly detection algorithms to monitor key performance indicators (KPIs) such as click-through rates, conversion rates, and ad engagement metrics. By detecting and addressing anomalies in real time, advertisers can mitigate risks, protect ad spend, and maintain campaign integrity.

Benefits of Advanced Analytics:

Advanced analytics techniques offer several benefits to AdTech companies and advertisers;

Improved Decision-Making: By leveraging predictive modeling and segmentation analysis, advertisers can make data-driven decisions that optimize ad targeting strategies and improve campaign performance.
Enhanced Audience Targeting: Segmentation analysis enables advertisers to understand their audience better and deliver personalized ad experiences that resonate with specific audience segments.

Risk Mitigation: Anomaly detection helps advertisers detect and address fraudulent activity or anomalous behavior in real time, minimizing the impact on campaign performance and ad spending.
Increased ROI: By utilizing advanced analytics to optimize ad targeting, advertisers can achieve higher conversion rates, lower acquisition costs, and ultimately, increase return on investment (ROI).

Advanced analytics techniques such as predictive modeling, segmentation analysis, and anomaly detection are essential tools for extracting actionable insights from data within the AdTech industry. By leveraging these techniques, AdTech companies can optimize ad targeting strategies, personalize ad experiences, and mitigate risks, ultimately driving better outcomes for advertisers and improving the effectiveness of digital advertising campaigns. As the AdTech landscape continues to evolve, the role of advanced analytics in informing decision-making and driving innovation will become increasingly prominent.

ENSURING DATA QUALITY, PRIVACY, & COMPLIANCE

Ensuring data quality, privacy, and compliance is of utmost importance for AdTech companies operating in a highly regulated environment. This section delves into the critical aspects of maintaining data integrity, protecting user privacy, and complying with relevant regulations such as the General Data Protection Regulation (GDPR) and the California Consumer Privacy Act (CCPA) within the AdTech industry.

1. Data Protection Regulations:
AdTech companies are subject to stringent data protection regulations that govern the collection, use, and sharing of personal data. GDPR, applicable to European Union (EU) residents, and CCPA, applicable to California residents, impose strict requirements on how personal data is

processed, stored, and protected. Advertisers must obtain explicit consent from users before collecting their data and ensure transparent data practices, including providing users with options to opt out of data collection and processing.

2. Role of Data Scientists:
Data scientists play a pivotal role in implementing data anonymization techniques, encryption methods, and access controls to safeguard sensitive information and mitigate the risk of data breaches. They work closely with cross-functional teams, including legal and compliance departments, to ensure that data processing activities comply with regulatory requirements. Data scientists also conduct privacy impact assessments and risk assessments to identify potential vulnerabilities and implement appropriate safeguards to protect user privacy.

3. Data Quality Assurance:
Maintaining data quality is essential for ensuring the accuracy, completeness, and consistency of data within AdTech platforms. Data quality assurance processes, such as data validation, cleansing, and deduplication, help identify and rectify errors, inconsistencies, and duplicates in the data. AdTech companies utilize automated data quality tools and algorithms to validate data inputs, enforce data integrity constraints, and monitor data quality metrics in real time. By ensuring data quality, advertisers can make informed decisions based on reliable and trustworthy data.

4. Transparency and Accountability:
Transparency and accountability are key principles in data privacy and compliance. AdTech companies are required to provide users with clear and concise privacy notices that explain how their data is collected, used, and shared. They must also maintain detailed records of data processing activities, including data sources, processing purposes, and data sharing practices, to demonstrate compliance with

regulatory requirements. Advertisers should implement mechanisms for users to exercise their data rights, such as the right to access, rectify, or delete their data.

5. Continuous Monitoring and Compliance:
AdTech companies employ continuous monitoring mechanisms to track data processing activities and ensure ongoing compliance with data protection regulations. They conduct regular audits and assessments to evaluate compliance with GDPR, CCPA, and other applicable regulations and address any identified deficiencies promptly. Data breach response plans and incident management procedures are established to mitigate the impact of security incidents and ensure timely notification to affected individuals and regulatory authorities.

Ensuring data quality, privacy, and compliance is a multifaceted endeavor that requires collaboration across organizational functions and adherence to best practices and regulatory standards. By implementing robust data protection measures, maintaining data quality assurance processes, and fostering transparency and accountability, AdTech companies can build trust with users, mitigate risks, and navigate the complex regulatory landscape effectively. As data privacy regulations continue to evolve, maintaining a proactive approach to data governance and compliance is essential for long-term success in the AdTech industry.

6. OPTIMIZING ADTECH PRODUCTS FOR SUCCESS

In the fiercely competitive landscape of digital advertising, optimizing AdTech products for success requires a multifaceted approach that encompasses continuous improvement, experimentation, performance monitoring, and adaptation to market trends and emerging technologies. This chapter explores key strategies and practices that AdTech professionals can employ to ensure the ongoing success and relevance of their products.

CONTINUOUS IMPROVEMENT & ITERATION

In today's fast-paced and ever-evolving landscape of AdTech (Advertising Technology), staying ahead of the curve is not just a competitive advantage; it's a necessity. The Agile approach to product management has emerged as a guiding philosophy for AdTech companies, providing a dynamic framework that enables them to thrive amidst the constantly shifting market dynamics and evolving user preferences.

At its core, Agile is all about embracing change, fostering collaboration, and delivering value incrementally. By breaking down the traditional linear product development process into small, manageable increments called sprints, Agile empowers AdTech teams to adapt quickly to emerging opportunities and challenges. Let's delve deeper into how the Agile approach facilitates continuous improvement and iteration within the context of AdTech product management.

Agile Principles in Action:
1. Iterative Development: Agile encourages iterative development, where AdTech products are built incrementally

in short cycles known as sprints, typically lasting 1-4 weeks. This iterative approach allows teams to release new features and updates frequently, gather user feedback, and incorporate insights into subsequent iterations.

2. Cross-Functional Collaboration: Agile promotes cross-functional collaboration among various stakeholders, including product managers, developers, designers, data scientists, marketers, and customer support representatives. By fostering a culture of collaboration and shared ownership, Agile teams can leverage diverse perspectives and expertise to drive innovation and deliver customer value.

3. User-Centric Design: Agile places a strong emphasis on understanding and addressing user needs and preferences. Through techniques such as user research, user story mapping, and persona development, AdTech teams gain deep insights into their target audience, enabling them to design and prioritize features that resonate with users and drive engagement.

4. Adaptive Planning: Agile embraces adaptive planning over rigid, upfront planning. Instead of trying to predict every detail of the product roadmap upfront, Agile teams prioritize flexibility and responsiveness, adapting their plans based on changing market conditions, customer feedback, and emerging opportunities.

5. Continuous Feedback Loop: Agile promotes a continuous feedback loop, where feedback from stakeholders and end-users is solicited early and often throughout the product development lifecycle. This feedback-driven approach enables teams to validate assumptions, course-correct as needed, and ensure that the product remains aligned with user expectations and business objectives.

Key Components of Agile Product Management in AdTech:

1. Product Backlog Management: The product backlog serves as a dynamic repository of all desired features, enhancements, and bug fixes. Product managers work closely with stakeholders to prioritize items in the backlog based on factors such as business value, user impact, and technical feasibility.

2. Sprint Planning and Execution: At the start of each sprint, Agile teams conduct sprint planning sessions to select a subset of items from the product backlog and define the goals and deliverables for the sprint. During the sprint, team members collaborate to design, develop, test, and deploy the selected features, with daily stand-up meetings to monitor progress and address any impediments.

3. Review and Retrospective: At the end of each sprint, Agile teams hold sprint review meetings to demonstrate the completed work to stakeholders and gather feedback. Concurrently, they conduct sprint retrospective sessions to reflect on what went well, what could be improved, and action items for future sprints, fostering a culture of continuous learning and improvement.

4. Minimum Viable Product (MVP) Approach: Agile encourages the development of Minimum Viable Products (MVPs) - stripped-down versions of the product that contain the essential features needed to address user needs and validate key assumptions. MVPs allow AdTech companies to test hypotheses, gather real-world feedback, and iterate rapidly based on user insights.

5. Data-Driven Decision Making: Agile promotes data-driven decision-making by leveraging analytics, A/B testing, and user metrics to evaluate the effectiveness of features and inform product direction. By analyzing user behavior, engagement metrics, and performance indicators, product

managers can make informed decisions about feature prioritization and optimization.

Benefits of the Agile Approach in AdTech Product Management:
1. Rapid Time-to-Market: Agile enables AdTech companies to accelerate time-to-market by delivering value incrementally and responding quickly to market demands and competitive pressures.

2. Enhanced Flexibility and Adaptability: Agile fosters a culture of adaptability and resilience, allowing AdTech teams to pivot in response to changing market conditions, emerging trends, and shifting user preferences.

3. Improved Product Quality: By emphasizing continuous testing, feedback, and refinement, Agile helps AdTech companies deliver higher-quality products that meet user needs and exceed expectations.

4. Increased Stakeholder Satisfaction: Agile promotes transparency, collaboration, and stakeholder engagement, resulting in greater satisfaction among customers, partners, and internal stakeholders.

5. Continuous Innovation and Learning: Agile empowers AdTech teams to experiment, innovate, and learn from failures, driving continuous improvement and innovation in product development.

The Agile approach to product management provides AdTech companies with a robust framework for continuous improvement and iteration, enabling them to navigate the complexities of the digital advertising landscape with agility, resilience, and innovation. By embracing Agile principles and practices, AdTech companies can stay ahead of the curve, delight customers, and drive business growth in an ever-evolving marketplace.

EXPERIMENTATION AND A/B TESTING FOR OPTIMIZATION

In the fast-paced world of AdTech, where the digital advertising landscape is constantly evolving, the ability to optimize products and campaigns is crucial for staying competitive and maximizing ROI. Experimentation and A/B testing have emerged as indispensable tools for AdTech companies, enabling them to fine-tune their products, ad creatives, and campaign strategies through iterative testing and data-driven insights.

Understanding Experimentation and A/B Testing:

1. Experimentation Framework: A/B testing is a method of experimentation where two or more variants (A and B) of a product feature, ad creative, or campaign element are compared to determine which performs better against predefined metrics. These experiments are typically conducted using controlled environments to isolate the impact of specific changes and gather statistically significant results.

2. Hypothesis Formulation: Before conducting an A/B test, AdTech teams formulate hypotheses based on insights from user research, market analysis, and past performance data. These hypotheses articulate the expected impact of the proposed changes on user behavior, engagement metrics, or conversion rates.

3. Variable Testing: A/B tests can be applied to various aspects of AdTech products and campaigns, including website layouts, call-to-action buttons, ad copy, targeting parameters, bidding strategies, and more. By testing different variables, advertisers can identify the most effective combinations and optimize performance accordingly.

Implementing A/B Testing in AdTech:
1. A/B Testing Platforms: AdTech companies leverage specialized A/B testing platforms and tools to design experiments, allocate traffic to different variants, track user interactions, and analyze results. These platforms provide intuitive interfaces, statistical analysis capabilities, and integration with analytics and ad-serving systems.

2. Controlled Experimentation: A/B tests are typically conducted in controlled environments where users are randomly assigned to different variants and their interactions are monitored and measured. This controlled setup ensures that external factors do not influence the outcomes of the experiments, allowing for an accurate assessment of the impact of the tested variables.

3. Statistical Analysis: A/B testing relies on statistical analysis techniques to determine the significance of observed differences between variants. Metrics such as conversion rates, click-through rates, engagement times, and revenue per user are compared using statistical tests to assess whether the observed differences are statistically significant.

Iterative Optimization and Continuous Improvement:
1. Data-Driven Insights: A/B testing generates valuable data and insights that inform decision-making and product optimization efforts. By analyzing the results of experiments, AdTech teams gain a deeper understanding of user preferences, behaviors, and pain points, allowing them to iterate on their products iteratively.

2. Iterative Testing: A/B testing is an iterative process, where findings from previous experiments inform the design of subsequent tests. AdTech teams continuously test and refine different hypotheses, gradually optimizing their products and campaigns based on empirical evidence and user feedback.

3. Continuous Learning: A/B testing fosters a culture of continuous learning and experimentation within AdTech organizations. By embracing a mindset of curiosity and exploration, advertisers can uncover new insights, discover untapped opportunities, and stay ahead of the competition in a rapidly evolving landscape.

Benefits of A/B Testing in AdTech:
1. Optimized Performance: A/B testing allows AdTech companies to identify and implement changes that lead to improved user engagement, higher conversion rates, and increased ROI for advertisers.

2. Data-Driven Decision Making: A/B testing enables advertisers to make informed decisions based on empirical evidence rather than intuition or guesswork, reducing the risk of costly mistakes and missed opportunities.

3. Iterative Improvement: A/B testing facilitates continuous improvement by providing a systematic framework for testing hypotheses, iterating on products, and refining strategies over time.

4. Personalized Experiences: A/B testing enables advertisers to tailor their products and campaigns to the preferences and behaviors of different audience segments, delivering personalized experiences that drive higher engagement and loyalty.

5. Competitive Advantage: By embracing A/B testing and optimization, AdTech companies can gain a competitive advantage in the market by staying agile, responsive, and innovative in their approach to product development and advertising strategies.

Experimentation and A/B testing are indispensable tools for optimizing AdTech products and maximizing their effectiveness in today's competitive landscape. By systematically testing hypotheses, analyzing data, and iterating on their products based on empirical evidence, advertisers can drive tangible results, enhance user experiences, and stay ahead of the curve in an ever-evolving digital ecosystem.

KEY METRICS AND KPI'S

In the dynamic and fast-paced world of AdTech, where advertising strategies evolve rapidly and user behavior is constantly changing, monitoring and measuring product performance are essential for driving success and staying ahead of the competition. Advertisers rely on a diverse set of key performance indicators (KPIs) to evaluate the effectiveness of their campaigns and inform strategic decision-making. Let's delve deeper into the key metrics and KPIs used in AdTech product management and how they contribute to continuous improvement and iteration within the Agile framework.

Understanding Key Metrics and KPIs in AdTech:
1. Click-Through Rate (CTR): CTR measures the percentage of users who click on an ad after seeing it. It indicates the effectiveness of ad creative, messaging, and targeting in capturing user attention and driving engagement.

2. Conversion Rate: The conversion rate represents the percentage of users who take a desired action after clicking on an ad, such as making a purchase, signing up for a newsletter, or completing a form. It reflects the effectiveness of the ad in driving desired outcomes and generating tangible results for advertisers.
3. Return on Ad Spend (ROAS): ROAS measures the revenue generated for every dollar spent on advertising. It provides insights into the efficiency and profitability of advertising

campaigns, helping advertisers optimize their budget allocation and maximize ROI.

4. Customer Acquisition Cost (CAC): CAC calculates the average cost of acquiring a new customer through advertising efforts. It includes expenses such as ad spend, campaign management fees, and creative production costs. By comparing CAC to customer lifetime value (CLV), advertisers can assess the sustainability and profitability of their customer acquisition strategies.

5. Engagement Metrics: Engagement metrics, such as time spent on site, page views per session, and bounce rate, provide insights into user engagement and interaction with ad content. These metrics help advertisers gauge the relevance and effectiveness of their ads in capturing user interest and driving meaningful interactions.

6. Reach and Impressions: Reach measures the total number of unique users exposed to an ad, while impressions represent the total number of times an ad is displayed. Reach and impressions metrics provide visibility into the audience reach and campaign exposure, informing advertisers about the scale and visibility of their ad campaigns.

Implementing Monitoring and Measurement Practices:
1. Analytics Platforms: Advertisers leverage analytics platforms such as Google Analytics, Adobe Analytics, and Facebook Insights to track and analyze key metrics in real-time. These platforms provide comprehensive dashboards, reports, and visualization tools to monitor campaign performance and identify optimization opportunities.

2. Event Tracking and Conversion Tracking: AdTech companies implement event tracking and conversion tracking mechanisms to monitor user interactions and track conversion events across various touchpoints. By setting up

tracking pixels, tags, and custom events, advertisers can capture valuable data on user behavior and campaign performance.

3. A/B Testing and Experimentation: A/B testing and experimentation play a crucial role in monitoring product performance and optimizing advertising strategies. By testing different ad variations, targeting parameters, and bidding strategies, advertisers can identify high-performing tactics and iterate on their campaigns based on empirical evidence.

4. Attribution Modeling: Attribution modeling enables advertisers to attribute conversions and revenue to specific advertising channels and touchpoints along the user journey. By analyzing attribution data, advertisers gain insights into the contribution of each marketing channel to overall conversion metrics and ROI, informing budget allocation decisions.

Continuous Improvement and Iteration:
1. Data-Driven Decision Making: Monitoring and measuring product performance enable advertisers to make data-driven decisions and iterate on their advertising strategies based on empirical evidence. By analyzing key metrics and KPIs, advertisers can identify trends, patterns, and opportunities for optimization, driving continuous improvement in campaign performance.

2. Optimization Strategies: Armed with insights from monitoring and measurement practices, advertisers can implement optimization strategies to improve campaign effectiveness and efficiency. Whether it's adjusting targeting parameters, refining ad creatives, or reallocating budget to high-performing channels, continuous optimization is essential for maximizing ROI and achieving campaign objectives.

3. Agile Adaptation: The Agile approach to product management emphasizes adaptability and responsiveness to change. AdTech companies leverage monitoring and measurement practices to iterate on their products and campaigns iteratively, responding to shifting market dynamics, emerging trends, and user feedback in real time.

Benefits of Monitoring and Measuring Product Performance:
1. Improved Decision-Making: By tracking key metrics and KPIs, advertisers gain actionable insights that inform strategic decision-making and optimization efforts.

2. Optimized ROI: Monitoring and measuring product performance enables advertisers to identify inefficiencies, optimize resources, and maximize return on investment (ROI) for advertising spend.

3. Enhanced User Experience: By analyzing engagement metrics and user behavior, advertisers can tailor ad experiences to user preferences, delivering more relevant and personalized content that resonates with their audience.

4. Iterative Innovation: Monitoring and measurement practices fuel continuous innovation and iteration within AdTech organizations, driving product improvements and competitive differentiation in the market.

5. Strategic Alignment: Key metrics and KPIs help align advertising efforts with business objectives, ensuring that campaigns are aligned with overarching goals and contribute to long-term growth and success.

Monitoring and measuring product performance are essential practices for effective product management in AdTech. By tracking key metrics and KPIs, AdTech companies can gain valuable insights, optimize advertising strategies, and drive continuous improvement and iteration within the Agile framework. Through a data-driven approach to decision-making and optimization, advertisers can unlock new opportunities, drive meaningful results, and stay ahead of the curve in an ever-evolving digital landscape.

ADAPTING TO MARKET TRENDS & EMERGING TECHNOLOGIES

In the dynamic and ever-evolving realm of AdTech, the ability to adapt to market trends and embrace emerging technologies is not just a strategic advantage; it's a necessity for staying competitive and relevant in an increasingly crowded marketplace. Advertisers must navigate a landscape characterized by rapid technological advancements, shifting consumer behaviors, and evolving regulatory landscapes. By keeping a finger on the pulse of industry trends and proactively leveraging emerging technologies, AdTech companies can seize new opportunities, unlock growth potential, and deliver innovative solutions that drive value for advertisers and consumers alike.

Understanding Market Trends and Technological Shifts:
1. Mobile Advertising Revolution: The proliferation of smartphones and mobile devices has transformed the advertising landscape, creating new opportunities and challenges for AdTech companies. Mobile advertising has emerged as a dominant force, with consumers spending more time on their mobile devices than ever before. Advertisers must prioritize mobile-first strategies, including responsive ad formats, location-based targeting, and in-app advertising, to reach audiences effectively in a mobile-centric world.

2. Rise of Programmatic Buying: Programmatic advertising has revolutionized the way ads are bought and sold, enabling real-time, automated transactions based on data-driven

insights. Programmatic platforms leverage artificial intelligence, machine learning, and data analytics to optimize ad targeting, placement, and pricing, resulting in greater efficiency, transparency, and scalability for advertisers. AdTech companies must embrace programmatic buying and invest in advanced targeting capabilities to remain competitive in today's digital advertising ecosystem.

3. Innovative Ad Formats: As consumer attention spans shrink and ad fatigue grows, advertisers are increasingly exploring innovative ad formats to capture audience attention and drive engagement. Interactive ads, immersive experiences, and rich media formats such as video, carousel ads, and augmented reality (AR) experiences are gaining traction, offering advertisers new ways to tell compelling stories and connect with consumers on a deeper level. AdTech companies must innovate and experiment with creative ad formats to deliver memorable brand experiences and differentiate themselves in a crowded marketplace.

4. Data Privacy and Compliance: With increasing scrutiny on data privacy and consumer protection, AdTech companies must navigate a complex regulatory landscape and ensure compliance with evolving regulations such as the General Data Protection Regulation (GDPR), California Consumer Privacy Act (CCPA), and upcoming changes like the proposed updates to Apple's App Tracking Transparency (ATT) framework. Advertisers must prioritize data privacy, transparency, and consent management to build trust with consumers and mitigate regulatory risks.

Strategies for Adapting to Market Trends and Emerging Technologies:
1. Continuous Market Research: AdTech companies must conduct ongoing market research and competitive analysis to stay informed about industry trends, consumer behaviors, and competitor strategies. By monitoring industry

publications, attending conferences, and engaging with industry experts, advertisers can gain valuable insights into emerging opportunities and potential threats.

2. Investment in R&D: Investing in research and development (R&D) is essential for staying at the forefront of technological innovation in AdTech. AdTech companies must allocate resources to explore emerging technologies such as artificial intelligence, machine learning, blockchain, and immersive media, and evaluate their potential applications in advertising and marketing.

3. Agile Product Development: Adopting an agile approach to product development enables AdTech companies to iterate quickly, respond to market feedback, and adapt to changing customer needs. By breaking down product development into small, manageable sprints, advertisers can prioritize features, test hypotheses, and deliver value to customers more efficiently.

4. Strategic Partnerships and Collaborations: Collaborating with strategic partners, including technology vendors, media companies, data providers, and creative agencies, can help AdTech companies access complementary expertise, resources, and distribution channels. Partnerships enable advertisers to leverage synergies, accelerate innovation, and address market gaps more effectively.

5. Talent Acquisition and Training: Building a skilled workforce equipped with the knowledge and expertise to navigate emerging technologies is critical for AdTech companies. Investing in talent acquisition, training programs, and skill development initiatives ensures that teams are equipped to leverage new technologies, drive innovation, and deliver value to customers.

Case Studies and Success Stories:
1. Snapchat's AR Lenses: Snapchat's AR lenses have transformed the way users interact with advertising content, enabling brands to create immersive, interactive experiences that drive engagement and brand awareness. By embracing AR technology, Snapchat has differentiated itself in the competitive social media landscape and attracted advertisers seeking innovative ad formats.

2. Google's Responsive Search Ads: Google's responsive search ads (RSAs) use machine learning algorithms to dynamically adjust ad copy and creative elements based on user queries and audience preferences. By automating ad customization and optimization, RSAs enable advertisers to deliver more relevant and personalized ad experiences, driving higher click-through rates and conversion rates.

3. Amazon's Programmatic Advertising Platform: Amazon's programmatic advertising platform leverages its vast trove of consumer data and advanced targeting capabilities to deliver highly targeted and personalized ads across its ecosystem of websites, apps, and devices. By offering advertisers access to rich audience insights and predictive analytics, Amazon's programmatic platform enables advertisers to reach high-intent shoppers and drive sales efficiently.

Adapting to market trends and embracing emerging technologies is essential for AdTech companies looking to stay competitive and drive innovation in today's dynamic landscape. By staying agile, proactive, and customer-centric, advertisers can seize new opportunities, address evolving consumer needs, and deliver impactful advertising solutions that resonate with audiences. Through continuous investment in R&D, strategic partnerships, and talent development, AdTech companies can position themselves for long-term success and leadership in the ever-evolving world of digital advertising.

7. FUTURE TRENDS & PREDICTIONS FOR ADTECH

The future of AdTech promises to be both exhilarating and challenging as emerging technologies and evolving consumer behaviors reshape the digital advertising landscape. In this chapter, we delve into the anticipated trends and predictions that will shape the future of AdTech, focusing on the role of AI, ML, data science, and emerging technologies in driving innovation and addressing the evolving needs of advertisers and consumers.

OPPORTUNITIES AND CHALLENGES

As we look ahead to the future of AdTech, it's clear that artificial intelligence (AI), machine learning (ML), and data science will play an increasingly pivotal role in shaping the landscape of digital advertising. These transformative technologies offer advertisers unprecedented opportunities to optimize targeting, personalize ad experiences, and measure campaign effectiveness like never before. However, with these opportunities also come significant challenges that must be addressed to ensure the ethical and responsible use of AI and data science in AdTech. Let's delve into the intricacies of the future of AI, ML, and data science in AdTech, exploring the vast potential and the pressing challenges that lie ahead.

Opportunities:
1. Optimized Targeting and Personalization: AI and ML algorithms will continue to revolutionize audience segmentation and targeting, enabling advertisers to deliver hyper-targeted and personalized ad experiences tailored to the unique preferences and behaviors of individual users. By

analyzing vast amounts of data in real time, AI-powered targeting algorithms can identify patterns, predict user intent, and optimize ad placements to maximize engagement and conversion rates.

2. Predictive Analytics and Forecasting: Data science techniques such as predictive modeling and advanced analytics will empower advertisers to extract actionable insights from complex datasets, enabling them to anticipate market trends, forecast campaign performance, and make data-driven decisions with confidence. By leveraging historical data and predictive algorithms, advertisers can optimize budget allocation, refine campaign strategies, and achieve better business outcomes.

3. Dynamic Creative Optimization: AI-driven dynamic creative optimization (DCO) platforms will enable advertisers to create highly personalized and contextually relevant ad creatives in real-time, based on user demographics, interests, and browsing behavior. By dynamically assembling ad elements such as images, headlines, and call-to-action buttons, DCO technology can deliver customized ad experiences that resonate with individual users and drive higher engagement and conversion rates.

4. Automated Campaign Management: AI-powered automation tools will streamline campaign management processes, allowing advertisers to automate routine tasks such as ad placement, bid optimization, and performance tracking. By harnessing the power of ML algorithms, advertisers can achieve greater efficiency, scalability, and ROI, freeing up valuable time and resources to focus on strategic initiatives and creative ideation.

Challenges:

1. Data Privacy and Consent Management: The proliferation of AI and data science in AdTech raises concerns about data privacy, consent management, and user tracking practices. Advertisers must navigate regulatory requirements such as GDPR, CCPA, and upcoming changes to Apple's App Tracking Transparency (ATT) framework, ensuring that user privacy is protected, and data handling practices are transparent and compliant.

2. Ad Fraud and Invalid Traffic: The rise of AI-driven ad targeting has also led to an increase in ad fraud and invalid traffic, posing significant challenges for advertisers seeking to maintain the integrity and effectiveness of their campaigns. Advertisers must implement robust fraud detection mechanisms, leverage blockchain technology for transparency and accountability, and collaborate with industry partners to combat ad fraud and ensure a level playing field for all stakeholders.

3. Algorithmic Bias and Fairness: ML algorithms are susceptible to biases inherent in the data they are trained on, leading to concerns about algorithmic bias and fairness in ad targeting and decision-making processes. Advertisers must proactively address biases in their data and algorithms, implement algorithmic fairness frameworks and auditing processes, and prioritize diversity and inclusivity in their advertising strategies to mitigate the risk of unintended discrimination and harm.

4. Transparency and Accountability: As AI and ML algorithms become increasingly complex and opaque, ensuring transparency and accountability in ad targeting practices becomes paramount. Advertisers must provide clear explanations of how AI-driven targeting algorithms work, disclose the sources of data used for targeting, and enable

users to understand and control their ad preferences and privacy settings effectively.

Ethical Considerations and Responsible AI:
1. Ethical Advertising Practices: Advertisers must adhere to ethical advertising practices and principles, ensuring that ads are truthful, transparent, and respectful of user preferences and rights. By prioritizing ethical considerations in ad targeting, advertisers can build trust with consumers, enhance brand reputation, and foster positive relationships with their audience.

2. Responsible AI Development: AdTech companies must adopt responsible AI development practices, including ethical design, bias mitigation, and algorithmic transparency. By embedding ethical considerations into the design and development of AI systems, advertisers can minimize the risk of unintended consequences and ensure that AI-driven ad targeting remains ethical, fair, and accountable.

3. User Empowerment and Control: Empowering users with greater control over their ad preferences and privacy settings is essential for fostering trust and transparency in the AdTech ecosystem. Advertisers must provide users with clear and accessible tools to opt out of targeted advertising, manage their data preferences, and exercise control over the ads they see online.

Collaborative Efforts and Industry Initiatives:
1. Cross-Industry Collaboration: Addressing the challenges and ethical considerations of AI and data science in AdTech requires collaborative efforts and industry-wide initiatives. Advertisers, technology providers, regulators, and advocacy groups must collaborate to develop best practices, standards, and guidelines for responsible AI and data usage in advertising.

2. Industry Self-Regulation: AdTech industry associations and consortiums can play a crucial role in promoting responsible AI and data practices through self-regulatory frameworks and industry guidelines. By establishing ethical standards and accountability mechanisms, industry organizations can help foster trust and integrity in the AdTech ecosystem.

3. Education and Awareness: Educating stakeholders about the opportunities and challenges of AI and data science in AdTech is essential for driving responsible innovation and adoption. Advertisers, policymakers, and consumers must be informed about the ethical considerations, privacy implications, and societal impacts of AI-driven advertising, enabling informed decision-making and responsible use of technology.

The future of AI, ML, and data science in AdTech holds tremendous promise for advertisers seeking to optimize targeting, personalize ad experiences, and measure campaign effectiveness.

However, realizing this potential requires a concerted effort to address the ethical considerations, privacy concerns, and challenges associated with AI-driven advertising. By embracing responsible AI development practices, promoting transparency and accountability, and fostering collaborative efforts across the industry, AdTech companies can harness the transformative power of AI and data science to create a more ethical, inclusive, and trustworthy advertising ecosystem for all stakeholders.

EMERGING TECHNOLOGIES & INNOVATIONS SHAPING THE FUTURE

The future of digital advertising is brimming with potential, driven by a diverse array of emerging technologies and innovations that promise to reshape the way advertisers connect with consumers and deliver compelling brand experiences. From immersive augmented reality (AR) and virtual reality (VR) to conversational AI and blockchain, these transformative trends hold the key to unlocking new opportunities for engagement, personalization, and transparency in the digital advertising ecosystem. Let's explore each of these emerging technologies in detail and their implications for the future of digital advertising.

Augmented Reality (AR) and Virtual Reality (VR):
1. Immersive Brand Experiences: AR and VR technologies enable advertisers to create immersive and interactive brand experiences that transcend traditional advertising formats. From virtual product demonstrations and 360-degree tours to gamified experiences and interactive storytelling, AR and VR offer a new dimension of engagement that captivates audiences and fosters deeper brand connections.

2. Enhanced Product Visualization: AR and VR empower consumers to visualize products in real-world contexts, allowing them to try before they buy and make more informed purchasing decisions. Advertisers can leverage AR try-on experiences, virtual showrooms, and product configurators to showcase products in immersive environments, enhancing the shopping experience and driving conversion rates.

3. Location-Based Advertising: AR-powered location-based advertising enables advertisers to deliver contextually relevant ads based on users' geographic location and surroundings. Whether it's overlaying digital signage in augmented reality or geo-targeting virtual experiences to specific locations, AR opens up new opportunities for hyper-localized advertising that resonates with consumers in their immediate environment.

Voice Search and Conversational AI:

1. Natural Language Interactions: Voice search and conversational AI technologies enable advertisers to engage with consumers through natural language interactions, mimicking human conversation and providing personalized responses to user queries. By integrating voice-enabled assistants and chatbots into their advertising strategies, advertisers can deliver tailored recommendations, answer customer inquiries, and facilitate voice-activated commerce seamlessly.

2. Personalized Recommendations: Conversational AI algorithms analyze user interactions and preferences to deliver personalized recommendations and suggestions in real time. Advertisers can leverage conversational data to understand user intent, anticipate needs, and recommend relevant products or services, driving higher engagement and conversion rates through conversational advertising experiences.

3. Voice-Activated Commerce: Voice commerce is poised to revolutionize the way consumers shop online, allowing users to make purchases and complete transactions using voice commands. Advertisers can integrate voice-enabled payment gateways and shopping assistants into their advertising platforms, streamlining the purchase process and enabling frictionless transactions through voice-activated commerce experiences.

Blockchain Technology:

1. Transparency and Accountability: Blockchain technology provides a transparent, secure, and decentralized framework for ad verification, fraud detection, and data management. By leveraging blockchain-based platforms, advertisers can ensure greater transparency and accountability in ad transactions, trace the provenance of ad impressions, and verify the authenticity of ad inventory and traffic sources.

2. Ad Fraud Prevention: Blockchain-based solutions offer robust mechanisms for detecting and preventing ad fraud, including invalid traffic, bot activity, and click fraud. By recording ad transactions on a distributed ledger and implementing consensus mechanisms, advertisers can mitigate the risk of fraudulent activity and ensure the integrity of the digital advertising supply chain.

3. Data Privacy and Consent Management: Blockchain enables users to maintain control over their personal data and privacy preferences through decentralized identity and consent management systems. Advertisers can leverage blockchain-based protocols to obtain user consent for data usage, track data permissions on a tamper-proof ledger, and ensure compliance with data protection regulations such as GDPR and CCPA.

Implications for Digital Advertising:
1. Enhanced Engagement and Interactivity: Emerging technologies such as AR, VR, and conversational AI offer advertisers new opportunities to engage with consumers through immersive, interactive, and personalized ad experiences that drive brand engagement and loyalty.

2. Improved Targeting and Personalization: Voice search and conversational AI algorithms enable advertisers to deliver more relevant and personalized ads based on user intent, preferences, and context, leading to higher conversion rates and ROI.

3. Greater Transparency and Trust: Blockchain technology provides advertisers with a transparent and decentralized framework for ad verification, fraud detection, and data management, enhancing trust and integrity in the digital advertising ecosystem.

4. Challenges and Considerations: While these emerging technologies hold immense potential for digital advertising, advertisers must also navigate challenges such as user privacy concerns, technical complexities, and regulatory compliance to realize the full benefits of these innovations responsibly.

The future of digital advertising is bright with possibilities, fueled by emerging technologies and innovations that promise to elevate the consumer experience, drive business outcomes, and transform the advertising landscape as we know it. By embracing these transformative trends and adapting their strategies accordingly, advertisers can position themselves for success in an increasingly digital and dynamic marketplace.

NEAR FUTURE PREDICTIONS FOR THE EVOLUTION OF ADTECH PRODUCTS

As we peer into the horizon of the digital advertising landscape, we discern a multitude of transformative trends and developments that will shape the evolution of AdTech platforms and products in the years ahead. From the proliferation of AI-powered personalization to the resurgence of contextual advertising and the growing emphasis on privacy-first strategies and sustainability, the future of AdTech is poised for innovation and adaptation to meet the changing needs and expectations of advertisers and consumers alike. Let's delve into each of these predictions in detail and explore their implications for the evolution of AdTech platforms and products.

AI-Powered Personalization:
1. Hyper-Targeted Ad Experiences: AI will continue to be a driving force behind the evolution of personalized advertising, empowering advertisers to deliver hyper-

targeted ad experiences that resonate with individual preferences and behaviors. By leveraging machine learning algorithms and predictive analytics, advertisers can analyze vast amounts of data to understand consumer intent, segment audiences, and tailor ad creative, messaging, and placement to maximize relevance and engagement.

2. Dynamic Content Optimization: AI-driven personalization extends beyond static ad targeting to dynamic content optimization, where ad elements such as images, headlines, and calls-to-action are dynamically customized based on real-time user interactions and context. Advertisers can deploy AI-powered content recommendation engines and dynamic creative optimization (DCO) platforms to deliver personalized ad experiences that adapt and evolve based on user preferences and behaviors, driving higher conversion rates and ROI.

Privacy-First Advertising:
1. User-Centric Data Practices: With the rise of privacy regulations such as GDPR, CCPA, and the impending demise of third-party cookies, advertisers will need to adopt privacy-first advertising strategies that prioritize user consent, transparency, and control over data usage. Advertisers must implement robust consent management platforms, obtain explicit user consent for data collection and targeting, and provide clear opt-out mechanisms to respect user privacy preferences while still delivering relevant and engaging ad experiences.

2. Contextual Targeting and Cohort Analysis: In the absence of individual user data, advertisers will increasingly turn to contextual advertising and cohort analysis as alternative targeting methods. By leveraging contextual signals such as content, context, and sentiment, advertisers can infer user intent and interests without relying on personally identifiable

information (PII), enabling them to deliver more relevant ads in a privacy-compliant manner.

Contextual Advertising:
1. Resurgence of Contextual Targeting: Contextual advertising will experience a resurgence as advertisers seek alternative targeting methods in response to privacy concerns and regulatory changes. By analyzing the context and content of web pages, apps, and digital environments, advertisers can identify relevant ad placements that align with user interests and intent, ensuring that ads are delivered in a brand-safe and contextually relevant environment.

2. Semantic Analysis and Natural Language Processing (NLP): Advertisers will leverage semantic analysis and natural language processing (NLP) technologies to extract insights from textual content and understand the context and sentiment of digital environments. By analyzing the semantics of web pages, social media posts, and other digital content, advertisers can identify relevant keywords, topics, and themes to inform contextual targeting and placement decisions, enhancing the relevance and effectiveness of their ad campaigns.

Cross-Channel Integration:
1. Holistic Advertising Strategies: Advertisers will adopt cross-channel advertising strategies that span multiple platforms, channels, and devices, enabling them to reach consumers wherever they are in their digital journey. By integrating data and insights from various touchpoints, including search, social media, display, and video, advertisers can deliver cohesive and personalized ad experiences that resonate with consumers across channels and drive omnichannel engagement and conversion.

2. Unified Measurement and Attribution: Cross-channel integration will also require unified measurement and attribution frameworks that enable advertisers to track and attribute conversions across multiple touchpoints accurately. By leveraging multi-touch attribution models, marketers can gain insights into the impact of each marketing channel on the customer journey and optimize budget allocation and campaign strategies accordingly, maximizing ROI and driving business outcomes.

Sustainability and Responsibility:
1. Brand Purpose and Values: Advertisers will place greater emphasis on sustainability and corporate responsibility in their advertising practices, aligning their brand messaging with values such as environmental stewardship, social justice, and diversity. By integrating purpose-driven messaging and cause-related marketing initiatives into their advertising campaigns, advertisers can resonate with socially conscious consumers and build brand loyalty and trust.

2. Ethical Advertising Practices: Advertisers will embrace ethical advertising practices that prioritize transparency, authenticity, and accountability in their communications with consumers. By adhering to industry best practices and standards, such as the Coalition for Better Ads (CBA) and the Interactive Advertising Bureau (IAB) guidelines, advertisers can foster a more transparent and trustworthy advertising ecosystem that benefits both brands and consumers alike.

The future of AdTech platforms and products is characterized by innovation, adaptation, and a renewed focus on user privacy, personalization, and responsibility. By embracing AI-powered personalization, privacy-first advertising strategies, contextual targeting, cross-channel integration, and sustainability, advertisers can navigate the evolving digital advertising landscape and deliver meaningful, relevant, and ethical ad experiences that resonate with consumers and drive business results. As the AdTech industry continues to evolve and mature, the possibilities for innovation and growth are endless, paving the way for a more dynamic, transparent, and impactful advertising ecosystem for all stakeholders.

8. USE CASES AND CASE STUDIES

In this chapter, we delve into real-world applications of AI, ML, and data science in AdTech, exploring how these technologies are transforming digital advertising and driving business outcomes. Through a series of use cases and case studies, we examine practical examples of targeted advertising, real-time bidding, content recommendation, predictive analytics, voice and visual search advertising, privacy-preserving AI solutions, and ethical considerations in AdTech.

Exploring the Practical Applications of AI, ML, & Data Science in AdTech

Before diving into specific use cases, we provide an overview of the practical applications of AI, ML, and data science in AdTech. From personalized ad targeting and bid optimization to content recommendation and predictive analytics, these technologies are revolutionizing the way advertisers reach and engage their target audiences.

TARGETED ADVERTISING: PERSONALIZING AD CONTENT & DELIVERY

Case Study 1: Dynamic Ad Creative Optimization Using Machine Learning Algorithms

In the dynamic realm of digital advertising, staying ahead of the curve requires innovative approaches to engage audiences effectively. One such strategy is dynamic ad creative optimization, where machine learning algorithms play a pivotal role in tailoring ad content to individual user preferences. In this case study, we delve into how a leading digital advertising platform harnesses machine learning to dynamically optimize ad creatives, thereby enhancing user engagement and maximizing return on investment (ROI).

Background:
Traditional advertising methods often rely on static ad creatives, which may lack relevance and fail to capture the attention of modern consumers. In contrast, dynamic ad creative optimization employs machine learning algorithms to analyze user data and adjust ad content in real-time based on user engagement metrics. This approach allows advertisers to deliver personalized and contextually relevant ad experiences, driving higher click-through rates (CTR), conversion rates, and overall campaign performance.

Implementation:
The implementation of dynamic ad creative optimization begins with the collection of user data, including demographic information, browsing behavior, and interaction history. This data is then fed into machine learning algorithms, which continuously analyze and learn from user interactions to identify patterns and preferences.

Using predictive modeling techniques, the machine learning algorithms predict which ad variations are most likely to resonate with individual users. These predictions inform real-time decisions about ad content, such as adjusting images, headlines, calls-to-action, and other creative elements to optimize user engagement.

Throughout the campaign lifecycle, the machine learning algorithms iteratively refine their predictions based on ongoing user feedback, ensuring that ad content remains relevant and effective across various audience segments and touchpoints.

Benefits:
Dynamic ad creative optimization offers several key benefits for advertisers:

1. Increased Relevance: By tailoring ad content to individual user preferences, advertisers can deliver more relevant and personalized ad experiences, increasing the likelihood of user engagement and conversion.

2. Improved Performance: Dynamic optimization allows advertisers to continuously iterate and refine ad creatives based on real-time data, leading to higher CTR, conversion rates, and overall campaign performance.

3. Enhanced Efficiency: Machine learning algorithms automate the process of ad creative optimization, eliminating the need for manual intervention and enabling advertisers to scale their campaigns more efficiently.

4. Better ROI: By maximizing the effectiveness of ad creatives, dynamic optimization helps advertisers achieve a higher return on investment (ROI) and allocate their advertising budgets more effectively.

Case Example:
Consider a clothing retailer launching a new digital advertising campaign to promote its latest collection. Using dynamic ad creative optimization, the retailer creates multiple ad variations showcasing different clothing items and styles.

As the campaign progresses, machine learning algorithms analyze user engagement metrics, such as clicks, conversions, and time spent on site, to determine which ad variations are resonating most with different audience segments.

Based on these insights, the algorithms automatically adjust ad content in real-time, highlighting the most popular clothing items and optimizing creative elements to maximize user engagement.

As a result, the retailer experiences a significant increase in CTR, conversion rates, and sales, ultimately achieving a higher ROI compared to traditional static ad campaigns.

Conclusion:
Dynamic ad creative optimization represents a powerful strategy for advertisers looking to enhance user engagement and drive better campaign performance. By harnessing the capabilities of machine learning algorithms, advertisers can deliver personalized and contextually relevant ad experiences that captivate audiences and deliver measurable results. As the digital advertising landscape continues to evolve, dynamic optimization will play an increasingly important role in helping advertisers stay competitive and achieve their advertising objectives.

Case Study 2: Predictive Audience Segmentation for Tailored Ad Targeting

In the dynamic landscape of targeted advertising, understanding and reaching the right audience is paramount for campaign success. Predictive audience segmentation leverages advanced analytics and machine learning algorithms to identify high-value audience segments based on past behavior, demographics, and interests. In this case study, we delve into how advertisers utilize predictive analytics to segment audiences effectively, enabling them to deliver personalized and targeted ad campaigns that resonate with their target audience.

Background:
Traditional audience segmentation methods often rely on basic demographic data, such as age, gender, and location. While useful, these static segmentation approaches may overlook nuances in user behavior and preferences. Predictive audience segmentation goes beyond demographics by analyzing historical data and applying machine learning algorithms to predict future behavior and

identify audience segments with the highest propensity to engage with specific ad campaigns.

Implementation:
The implementation of predictive audience segmentation begins with the collection of diverse data sources, including user interactions, browsing history, purchase behavior, and social media activity. This data is then processed and analyzed using predictive analytics techniques, such as clustering algorithms, decision trees, and neural networks.

Machine learning algorithms analyze historical data to identify patterns and correlations between user attributes and behavior. By identifying predictive features that are indicative of user engagement and conversion, these algorithms can segment audiences into distinct clusters or segments based on shared characteristics and behaviors.

Once audience segments are identified, advertisers can tailor their ad messaging, creative assets, and targeting strategies to align with the preferences and interests of each segment. This may involve creating personalized ad content, adjusting bid strategies, and selecting the most relevant ad placements and channels to reach each audience segment effectively.

Throughout the campaign lifecycle, machine learning algorithms continuously learn and adapt based on real-time feedback and performance metrics. This iterative process allows advertisers to refine their audience segmentation strategies over time, optimizing campaign effectiveness and driving higher conversion rates.

Benefits:
Predictive audience segmentation offers several key benefits for advertisers:

1. Enhanced Targeting Accuracy: By leveraging predictive analytics, advertisers can segment audiences more accurately based on past behavior and predicted future actions, enabling them to target users who are most likely to respond to specific ad campaigns.

2. Improved Campaign Relevance: Tailoring ad messaging and targeting strategies to the preferences and interests of each audience segment enhances campaign relevance and increases the likelihood of user engagement and conversion.

3. Increased Campaign Effectiveness: Predictive audience segmentation enables advertisers to allocate their advertising budgets more efficiently by focusing resources on high-value audience segments with the highest propensity to convert, resulting in higher ROI and campaign effectiveness.

4. Dynamic Adaptation: Machine learning algorithms continuously learn and adapt based on real-time data, allowing advertisers to refine their audience segmentation strategies over time and stay responsive to changing market dynamics and user behavior.

Case Example:
Consider an e-commerce retailer launching a new advertising campaign to promote its summer clothing collection. Using predictive audience segmentation, the retailer analyzes historical data to identify audience segments with a high likelihood of purchasing summer clothing items based on past behavior, such as browsing activity, previous purchases, and engagement with summer-related content.

Armed with insights from predictive analytics, the retailer tailors its ad messaging and targeting strategies to resonate with each audience segment. For example, users who have previously shown interest in beachwear may receive ads highlighting swimsuits and beach accessories, while users interested in outdoor activities may receive ads showcasing hiking gear and outdoor apparel.

As the campaign progresses, machine learning algorithms monitor user engagement and conversion rates, adjusting targeting strategies and creative assets in real-time to optimize campaign performance. By delivering personalized and relevant ad experiences to each audience segment, the retailer achieves higher conversion rates and ROI compared to traditional one-size-fits-all ad campaigns.

Conclusion:
Predictive audience segmentation represents a powerful tool for advertisers seeking to maximize the effectiveness of their targeted advertising campaigns. By leveraging advanced analytics and machine learning algorithms, advertisers can identify high-value audience segments, personalize ad messaging, and optimize targeting strategies to drive higher engagement and conversions. As the digital advertising landscape continues to evolve, predictive audience segmentation will play an increasingly important role in helping advertisers reach and resonate with their target audience effectively..

REAL-TIME BIDDING AND PROGRAMMATIC ADVERTISING

Case Study 3: Bid Optimization Strategies Using Predictive Analytics

Real-time bidding (RTB) and programmatic advertising have revolutionized the digital advertising landscape, allowing advertisers to bid on ad impressions in real-time and target users with unprecedented precision. In this case study, we delve into how advertisers leverage predictive analytics to optimize bidding strategies in real-time auction environments, maximizing ad impressions and minimizing costs to achieve more efficient and effective ad campaigns.

Background:
Real-time bidding (RTB) enables advertisers to bid on ad impressions in real-time, allowing them to reach target audiences across a vast network of websites and apps. Programmatic advertising platforms facilitate the buying and selling of ad inventory through automated bidding processes, connecting advertisers with publishers in milliseconds. Predictive analytics plays a crucial role in optimizing bidding strategies by analyzing historical bidding data and user behavior patterns to predict the likelihood of ad impressions converting into desired outcomes, such as clicks or conversions.

Implementation:
The implementation of bid optimization strategies using predictive analytics involves several key steps:

1. Data Collection: Advertisers collect vast amounts of historical bidding data, including bid prices, ad impressions, click-through rates (CTR), conversion rates, and user behavior patterns.

2. Data Analysis: Predictive analytics algorithms analyze historical bidding data to identify patterns and correlations between bidding strategies, user behavior, and campaign outcomes. Machine learning algorithms such as regression analysis, decision trees, and neural networks are used to predict the likelihood of ad impressions converting into desired outcomes.

3. Model Training: Machine learning models are trained using historical bidding data to predict the optimal bid price for each ad impression based on user behavior and campaign objectives. These models learn from past bidding strategies and user interactions to make accurate predictions in real-time.

4. Real-Time Bidding: During real-time auctions, advertisers use predictive analytics to dynamically adjust their bidding strategies based on the predicted likelihood of ad impressions converting into desired outcomes. Advertisers bid higher for ad impressions with a high probability of conversion and lower for ad impressions with a low probability, maximizing ad impressions while minimizing costs.

5. Performance Monitoring: Advertisers continuously monitor the performance of their bidding strategies in real-time, analyzing key metrics such as ad impressions, CTR, conversion rates, and return on investment (ROI). Machine learning algorithms iteratively refine bidding strategies based on real-time feedback, optimizing campaign performance over time.

Benefits:
Bid optimization strategies using predictive analytics offer several key benefits for advertisers:

1. Maximized Ad Impressions: By dynamically adjusting bidding strategies in real-time, advertisers can maximize ad impressions and reach their target audience more effectively.

2. Minimized Costs: Predictive analytics enables advertisers to bid more strategically, avoiding overpaying for ad impressions with a low likelihood of converting into desired outcomes, resulting in lower advertising costs.

3. Improved Campaign Performance: Optimized bidding strategies lead to improved campaign performance, with higher CTR, conversion rates, and ROI compared to traditional bidding approaches.

4. Efficient Resource Allocation: Predictive analytics helps advertisers allocate their advertising budgets more efficiently

by focusing resources on ad impressions with the highest probability of converting into desired outcomes, maximizing the return on investment.

Case Example:
Consider an e-commerce retailer launching a new advertising campaign to promote its latest product line. Using predictive analytics, the retailer analyzes historical bidding data to identify patterns and trends in user behavior and campaign performance.

Based on insights from predictive analytics, the retailer adjusts its bidding strategies in real-time during auctions, bidding higher for ad impressions with a high probability of resulting in conversions and lower for ad impressions with a low probability.

As the campaign progresses, the retailer continuously monitors the performance of its bidding strategies, optimizing bid prices and allocation of resources to maximize ad impressions and minimize costs.

Conclusion:
Bid optimization strategies using predictive analytics represent a powerful tool for advertisers seeking to maximize the effectiveness of their real-time bidding campaigns. By leveraging historical data and machine learning algorithms, advertisers can dynamically adjust bidding strategies in real-time to maximize ad impressions, minimize costs, and achieve better campaign performance. As the digital advertising landscape continues to evolve, predictive analytics will play an increasingly important role in helping advertisers optimize their bidding strategies and achieve their advertising objectives efficiently and effectively.

Case Study 4: Fraud Detection and Prevention in Programmatic Advertising

In the complex landscape of programmatic advertising, the rise of real-time bidding (RTB) has introduced new challenges, including the prevalence of ad fraud. Advertisers face the constant threat of fraudulent activities such as bot traffic, click fraud, and ad stacking, which can drain advertising budgets and undermine campaign effectiveness. In this case study, we explore how advertisers leverage machine learning algorithms to detect and prevent ad fraud in programmatic advertising, safeguarding their ad spending and maintaining campaign integrity.

Background:
Programmatic advertising automates the buying and selling of digital ad inventory through real-time auctions, allowing advertisers to reach target audiences with unprecedented precision. However, the anonymity and complexity of programmatic ad exchanges create opportunities for fraudsters to exploit vulnerabilities in the system and generate fake ad impressions and clicks for financial gain. Advertisers must implement robust fraud detection and prevention strategies to mitigate the risk of ad fraud and protect their advertising investments.

Implementation:
The implementation of fraud detection and prevention in programmatic advertising involves several key components:

1. Data Collection: Advertisers collect vast amounts of data from programmatic ad exchanges, including ad impressions, clicks, conversions, and user interactions. This data provides valuable insights into traffic patterns, user behavior, and campaign performance.

2. Anomaly Detection: Machine learning algorithms analyze historical data to identify patterns of suspicious activity and

anomalous behavior indicative of ad fraud. These algorithms leverage techniques such as clustering, regression analysis, and anomaly detection to detect deviations from normal traffic patterns and flag potentially fraudulent traffic sources.

3. Behavioral Analysis: Machine learning models analyze user behavior and engagement metrics to distinguish between legitimate and fraudulent traffic. By examining factors such as click-through rates (CTR), time on site, and conversion rates, these models can identify patterns associated with bot activity, click farms, and other forms of ad fraud.

4. Predictive Modeling: Machine learning algorithms use predictive modeling techniques to forecast the likelihood of ad fraud based on historical data and real-time indicators. These models assess the risk of individual ad impressions and clicks being fraudulent and assign a fraud score to each traffic source, allowing advertisers to prioritize resources and take proactive measures to mitigate fraud risk.

5. Real-Time Monitoring: Advertisers monitor programmatic ad campaigns in real-time, using machine learning algorithms to detect and respond to ad fraud as it occurs. Automated systems flag suspicious activity, such as sudden spikes in traffic or unusually high click-through rates, triggering immediate investigations and corrective actions.

Benefits:
Fraud detection and prevention in programmatic advertising offer several key benefits for advertisers:

1. Protect Ad Spend: By detecting and preventing ad fraud, advertisers can protect their advertising budgets from being wasted on fraudulent traffic sources, ensuring that their ad spend generates genuine engagement and ROI.

2. Maintain Campaign Integrity: Preventing ad fraud helps maintain the integrity of programmatic ad campaigns, preserving the credibility and effectiveness of advertising efforts and fostering trust between advertisers and publishers.

3. Enhance Brand Safety: Advertisers safeguard their brand reputation by ensuring that ads are served in brand-safe environments free from fraudulent activity, minimizing the risk of associating their brand with malicious or inappropriate content.

4. Optimize Campaign Performance: Fraud detection and prevention measures enable advertisers to optimize campaign performance by eliminating fraudulent traffic and focusing resources on high-quality ad impressions and clicks, leading to higher conversion rates and ROI.

Case Example:
Consider an online retailer running a programmatic advertising campaign to promote its new product line. Using machine learning algorithms for fraud detection and prevention, the retailer monitors campaign performance in real-time and detects suspicious activity, such as unusually high click-through rates from certain traffic sources.

Upon investigation, the retailer identifies these traffic sources as bots and takes immediate action to block them from accessing the campaign, preventing further ad fraud. As a result, the retailer protects its ad spend, maintains campaign integrity, and maximizes the effectiveness of its advertising efforts.

Conclusion:
Fraud detection and prevention are critical components of successful programmatic advertising campaigns. By leveraging machine learning algorithms to analyze patterns of suspicious activity and anomalous behavior, advertisers can

detect and mitigate ad fraud in real-time, safeguarding their ad spend and maintaining campaign integrity. As the digital advertising landscape continues to evolve, robust fraud detection and prevention strategies will remain essential for advertisers seeking to maximize the effectiveness and efficiency of their programmatic ad campaigns.

ATTRIBUTION MODELING AND CAMPAIGN OPTIMIZATION

Case Study 5: Multi-Touch Attribution Modeling for Cross-Channel Campaigns

In the modern marketing landscape, consumers interact with brands across multiple touchpoints before making a purchase decision. Multi-touch attribution modeling allows advertisers to accurately attribute conversions to each touchpoint in the customer journey, providing insights into the effectiveness of different marketing channels and campaigns. In this case study, we explore how advertisers leverage multi-touch attribution modeling to optimize their marketing mix and allocate budget more effectively to channels that drive the highest return on investment (ROI).

Background:
Traditionally, advertisers relied on single-touch attribution models, such as first-touch or last-touch attribution, which assign all credit for a conversion to a single touchpoint in the customer journey. However, these models fail to capture the complexity of modern consumer behavior, where customers interact with brands through multiple channels and devices before converting. Multi-touch attribution modeling addresses this challenge by analyzing the entire customer journey and assigning appropriate credit to each touchpoint based on its contribution to the conversion.

Implementation:

The implementation of multi-touch attribution modeling for cross-channel campaigns involves several key steps:

1. Data Integration: Advertisers collect data from various sources, including website analytics, ad platforms, CRM systems, and sales databases. This data provides a comprehensive view of the customer journey, tracking interactions across different touchpoints and channels.

2. Attribution Model Selection: Advertisers select an attribution model that best fits their business objectives and marketing goals. Common attribution models include linear, time decay, U-shaped, W-shaped, and custom models, each of which assigns credit to different touchpoints in the customer journey based on predefined rules or algorithms.

3. Data Analysis: Using statistical techniques and machine learning algorithms, advertisers analyze historical data to identify patterns and correlations between different touchpoints and conversion events. This analysis helps determine the relative impact of each touchpoint on the conversion and informs the attribution model's weighting scheme.

4. Model Training: Machine learning algorithms are trained using historical data to learn the relationships between touchpoints and conversions. These algorithms use supervised learning techniques to optimize the attribution model's parameters and improve its accuracy in predicting conversion probabilities based on past behavior.

5. Attribution Calculation: Once the attribution model is trained, advertisers use it to calculate the contribution of each touchpoint to the conversion. This involves applying the model's weighting scheme to the data collected from each touchpoint and aggregating the results to determine the

overall contribution of each channel and campaign to the conversion.

Benefits:
Multi-touch attribution modeling offers several key benefits for advertisers:

1. Improved Insights: By accurately attributing conversions to each touchpoint in the customer journey, advertisers gain deeper insights into the effectiveness of different marketing channels and campaigns, allowing them to make more informed decisions about resource allocation and campaign optimization.

2. Optimized Marketing Mix: Multi-touch attribution modeling helps advertisers optimize their marketing mix by identifying the most influential touchpoints and allocating budget more effectively to channels that drive the highest ROI. This leads to better overall campaign performance and higher return on investment.

3. Enhanced Campaign Optimization: Armed with insights from multi-touch attribution modeling, advertisers can optimize their campaigns in real-time, adjusting targeting, messaging, and creative assets to better engage with consumers at each stage of the customer journey.

4. Increased Accountability: By providing a transparent and data-driven view of the customer journey, multi-touch attribution modeling increases accountability and alignment between marketing efforts and business outcomes, fostering a culture of continuous improvement and optimization.

Case Example:
Consider an e-commerce retailer running a cross-channel marketing campaign to promote its new product launch. Using multi-touch attribution modeling, the retailer analyzes

the customer journey and identifies key touchpoints, including social media ads, search engine marketing, email newsletters, and website visits.

By attributing conversions to each touchpoint based on their contribution to the conversion, the retailer discovers that social media ads played a significant role in driving initial awareness, while search engine marketing and email newsletters were instrumental in driving consideration and purchase intent.

Armed with these insights, the retailer reallocates the budget from less effective channels to social media ads, search engine marketing, and email newsletters, resulting in higher conversion rates and ROI for the campaign.

Conclusion:
Multi-touch attribution modeling is a powerful tool for advertisers seeking to understand and optimize the effectiveness of their cross-channel marketing campaigns. By accurately attributing conversions to each touchpoint in the customer journey, advertisers can gain valuable insights into the impact of different marketing channels and campaigns, enabling them to allocate budget more effectively, optimize their marketing mix, and drive better overall campaign performance. As the digital advertising landscape continues to evolve, multi-touch attribution modeling will remain essential for advertisers looking to maximize the return on investment from their marketing efforts.

Case Study 6: Predictive Modeling for Campaign Performance Optimization
In the dynamic world of digital advertising, predicting campaign performance and optimizing marketing strategies are crucial for achieving success. Predictive modeling offers advertisers a powerful tool to forecast campaign outcomes and make data-driven decisions. In this case study, we delve

into how advertisers leverage predictive modeling to optimize campaign performance, utilizing historical data and external factors to drive better results and meet their business objectives.

Background:
Traditional campaign planning often relies on historical data and intuition to guide decision-making. However, the rapid pace of change in the digital advertising landscape demands more sophisticated approaches. Predictive modeling leverages advanced analytics and machine learning algorithms to analyze historical campaign data and external factors, such as seasonality and market trends, to forecast future performance accurately.

Implementation:
The implementation of predictive modeling for campaign performance optimization involves several key steps:

1. Data Collection: Advertisers gather historical campaign data, including ad impressions, clicks, conversions, and other relevant metrics. Additionally, they collect external data sources such as market trends, competitor activities, and economic indicators.

2. Feature Engineering: Advertisers preprocess and engineer features from the collected data to create meaningful predictors for the predictive model. These features may include campaign attributes, audience demographics, historical performance metrics, and external factors like weather or economic indicators.

3. Model Selection: Advertisers select appropriate predictive modeling techniques based on the nature of the data and the business objectives. Common predictive modeling algorithms include linear regression, decision trees, random forests, gradient boosting, and neural networks.

4. Model Training: Advertisers train the predictive model using historical campaign data and external factors. The model learns patterns and relationships in the data to make accurate predictions about future campaign performance.

5. Validation and Testing: Advertisers validate the predictive model using a holdout dataset to ensure its accuracy and generalizability. They also conduct rigorous testing to evaluate the model's performance under different scenarios and conditions.

6. Deployment and Optimization: Once validated, advertisers deploy the predictive model to forecast campaign performance in real time. They use the model's predictions to optimize marketing strategies, allocate budget effectively, and make data-driven decisions to maximize campaign effectiveness.

Benefits:
Predictive modeling for campaign performance optimization offers several key benefits for advertisers:

1. Improved Decision-Making: Predictive modeling provides advertisers with accurate forecasts of campaign performance, enabling them to make informed decisions and allocate resources more effectively.

2. Optimized Marketing Strategies: By leveraging predictive insights, advertisers can optimize their marketing strategies in real-time, adjusting targeting, messaging, and creative assets to maximize engagement and conversions.

3. Better Resource Allocation: Predictive modeling helps advertisers allocate budget and resources more efficiently, focusing investment on campaigns and channels with the highest predicted ROI.

4. Increased ROI: By optimizing marketing strategies and resource allocation, advertisers can achieve a higher return on investment (ROI) from their advertising efforts, driving business growth and success.

Case Example:
Consider a retail brand planning a holiday marketing campaign to drive sales during the festive season. Using predictive modeling, the brand analyzes historical campaign data, including past holiday campaigns' performance, customer behavior, and market trends.

The predictive model forecasts the expected performance of the upcoming holiday campaign based on historical data and external factors such as consumer sentiment, economic indicators, and competitor activities. The model predicts which marketing channels, messaging, and promotions are likely to drive the highest sales and ROI during the holiday season.

Armed with these insights, the retail brand optimizes its holiday marketing strategy, reallocating the budget to high-performing channels, refining messaging and creative assets, and adjusting targeting parameters to maximize engagement and conversions.

Conclusion:
Predictive modeling for campaign performance optimization is a valuable tool for advertisers seeking to maximize the effectiveness of their marketing efforts. By leveraging historical data and external factors, advertisers can forecast campaign performance accurately and make data-driven decisions to optimize marketing strategies, allocate resources more effectively, and achieve their business objectives. As the digital advertising landscape continues to evolve, predictive modeling will remain essential for advertisers

looking to stay ahead of the competition and drive better campaign results.

CONTENT RECOMMENDATION AND DISCOVERY

Case Study 7: Personalized Content Recommendations Using Collaborative Filtering

In the digital era, content recommendation and discovery play a pivotal role in engaging users and keeping them coming back to content platforms. Collaborative filtering algorithms offer a powerful solution to personalize content recommendations based on user's past behavior and preferences. In this case study, we delve into how publishers and content platforms leverage collaborative filtering to enhance user experience through personalized content recommendations.

Background:
Content recommendation systems aim to deliver relevant and engaging content to users based on their interests, preferences, and behavior. Collaborative filtering is a popular approach that leverages similarities between users or items to make personalized recommendations. By analyzing user interactions and content metadata, publishers can utilize collaborative filtering algorithms to suggest content that aligns with users' tastes and interests.

Implementation:
The implementation of personalized content recommendations using collaborative filtering involves several key steps:

1. Data Collection: Publishers gather data on user interactions with content, including clicks, views, likes, shares, and other engagement metrics. They also collect metadata about the content itself, such as genre, category, tags, and keywords.

2. User-item Matrix: Publishers construct a user-item matrix that represents the interactions between users and content. Each row of the matrix corresponds to a user, each column corresponds to an item (i.e., a piece of content), and the matrix cells contain the level of interaction between each user-item pair.

3. Similarity Calculation: Collaborative filtering algorithms compute similarities between users or items based on their interaction patterns. Various similarity metrics, such as cosine similarity, Pearson correlation coefficient, or Jaccard similarity, can be used to measure the similarity between user profiles or content items.

4. Recommendation Generation: Based on the computed similarities, the collaborative filtering algorithm generates personalized recommendations for each user. For user-based collaborative filtering, recommendations are made by identifying users with similar preferences and suggesting items they have interacted with but the target user has not. For item-based collaborative filtering, recommendations are made by identifying items similar to those the user has interacted with and suggesting them.

5. Ranking and Filtering: Publishers rank the recommended items based on relevance scores or predicted ratings and apply filtering criteria to ensure that only high-quality and relevant content is recommended to users. Filtering criteria may include factors such as content freshness, popularity, user feedback, and editorial guidelines.

Benefits:
Personalized content recommendations using collaborative filtering offer several key benefits for publishers and content platforms:

1. Enhanced User Engagement: By delivering personalized content recommendations tailored to users' interests and preferences, publishers can increase user engagement and retention, leading to longer session durations and higher page views.

2. Improved Content Discovery: Personalized recommendations help users discover new and relevant content that they may not have found otherwise, expanding their content consumption and driving exploration of the platform's content library.

3. Increased User Satisfaction: Personalized recommendations enhance user satisfaction by delivering content that aligns with their individual tastes and interests, fostering a positive user experience and strengthening brand loyalty.

4. Optimized Content Monetization: By increasing user engagement and retention, personalized content recommendations can drive higher ad impressions, click-through rates, and conversions, leading to increased advertising revenue and monetization opportunities for publishers.

Case Example:
Consider a streaming platform that offers a vast library of movies and TV shows. Using collaborative filtering, the platform analyzes user interactions with content, such as viewing history, ratings, and preferences.

Based on this data, the platform's recommendation system identifies users with similar tastes and recommends movies and TV shows that these users have enjoyed but the target user has not yet watched. Additionally, the system suggests similar items to those the user has interacted with, based on content metadata and user behavior patterns.

As a result, users receive personalized recommendations tailored to their individual preferences, leading to increased engagement, longer viewing sessions, and improved satisfaction with the platform's content offerings.

Conclusion:
Personalized content recommendations using collaborative filtering are a powerful tool for publishers and content platforms seeking to enhance user experience and drive engagement. By leveraging user interactions and content metadata, collaborative filtering algorithms can deliver tailored recommendations that align with users' tastes and preferences, leading to increased engagement, retention, and satisfaction. As the digital content landscape continues to evolve, personalized recommendation systems will remain essential for publishers looking to differentiate themselves and provide value to their audiences.

Case Study 8: AI-Powered Content Discovery Platforms for Publishers

In today's digital landscape, publishers face the challenge of capturing users' attention amidst the vast sea of content available online. AI-powered content discovery platforms offer a solution by leveraging advanced algorithms to surface relevant content to users in real time. In this case study, we explore how publishers harness AI technology to enhance content discovery, drive user engagement, and unlock monetization opportunities.

Background:
Content discovery platforms utilize artificial intelligence (AI) and machine learning (ML) algorithms to analyze user behavior, preferences, and contextual signals to deliver personalized content recommendations. By understanding user intent and leveraging contextual information, publishers can enhance the user experience by presenting relevant content tailored to each user's interests and needs.

Implementation:
The implementation of AI-powered content discovery platforms for publishers involves several key components:

1. Data Collection: Publishers collect data on user interactions, such as clicks, views, likes, shares, and dwell time, across their digital properties, including websites, mobile apps, and social media platforms. They also gather contextual data, such as location, device type, time of day, and browsing history.

2. AI Algorithms: Publishers deploy AI and ML algorithms to analyze the collected data and extract insights about user preferences, behavior patterns, and content relevance. These algorithms include collaborative filtering, content-based filtering, natural language processing (NLP), and deep learning models.

3. User Profiling: AI-powered content discovery platforms create user profiles based on historical behavior and real-time interactions. These profiles capture users' interests, preferences, and engagement patterns, allowing publishers to deliver personalized content recommendations tailored to each user.

4. Content Recommendation Engine: The content recommendation engine leverages AI algorithms to generate personalized recommendations for users in real time. By analyzing user profiles, content metadata, and contextual signals, the recommendation engine selects relevant content items and presents them to users through various channels, such as recommendation widgets, personalized feeds, and email newsletters.

5. Real-Time Optimization: Publishers continuously optimize the content discovery platform based on user feedback and performance metrics. AI algorithms analyze user engagement

data to refine recommendation models, adjust content weighting, and improve the accuracy of recommendations over time.

Benefits:
AI-powered content discovery platforms offer several key benefits for publishers:

1. Enhanced User Engagement: By delivering personalized content recommendations, publishers increase user engagement and time spent on their digital properties, leading to higher page views, ad impressions, and conversion rates.

2. Improved Content Monetization: Personalized content recommendations drive higher engagement and click-through rates, resulting in increased advertising revenue and monetization opportunities for publishers. Additionally, publishers can leverage AI insights to optimize ad placement, targeting, and pricing strategies.

3. Increased User Satisfaction: Personalized content recommendations improve the user experience by providing relevant and valuable content tailored to each user's interests and preferences. This enhances user satisfaction and loyalty, driving repeat visits and brand affinity.

4. Data-driven decision-making: AI-powered content discovery platforms provide publishers with actionable insights into user behavior, content performance, and audience segmentation. Publishers can use these insights to inform content strategy, editorial decisions, and marketing campaigns, maximizing the impact of their digital initiatives.

Case Example:
Consider a news publisher that operates a digital platform offering a wide range of articles, videos, and multimedia

content. Using an AI-powered content discovery platform, the publisher analyzes user behavior and preferences to deliver personalized content recommendations.

The AI algorithms analyze user interactions, such as article views, topic preferences, and engagement metrics, to create individual user profiles. Based on these profiles, the content discovery platform generates personalized recommendations for each user, suggesting articles, videos, and related content that align with their interests.

As a result, users receive a tailored content experience that reflects their unique preferences and browsing habits, leading to increased engagement, longer session durations, and higher satisfaction with the publisher's platform.

Conclusion:
AI-powered content discovery platforms offer publishers a powerful tool to enhance user engagement, drive monetization opportunities, and deliver personalized experiences at scale. By leveraging advanced AI algorithms to analyze user behavior and contextual signals, publishers can surface relevant content to users in real time, fostering deeper connections and driving business growth. As the digital content landscape continues to evolve, AI-powered content discovery platforms will play a central role in helping publishers stay ahead of the curve and deliver value to their audiences.

PREDICTIVE ANALYTICS FOR AUDIENCE INSIGHTS AND TRENDS

Case Study 9: Predictive Analytics for Audience Insights and Trends
In the realm of digital advertising, understanding user behavior and intent is paramount for advertisers seeking to create effective campaigns. Predictive analytics, powered by

machine learning models, offers a sophisticated approach to anticipate user actions based on historical data and contextual signals. In this case study, we delve into how advertisers leverage machine learning to predict user behavior and intent, enabling them to optimize ad targeting and messaging strategies for maximum impact.

Background:
Advertisers are constantly striving to deliver relevant and personalized ad experiences to their target audience. Predictive analytics enables advertisers to forecast user behavior and intent by analyzing historical data, such as past interactions, purchase history, and demographic information, along with contextual signals like device type, location, and time of day. By leveraging machine learning models, advertisers can uncover patterns and trends in user data to make informed predictions about future actions.

Implementation:
The implementation of predictive analytics for audience insights and trends involves the following steps:

1. Data Collection: Advertisers collect a diverse array of data sources, including website analytics, CRM systems, ad platforms, social media interactions, and third-party data providers. This data encompasses user interactions, demographic information, browsing behavior, purchase history, and other relevant attributes.

2. Feature Engineering: Advertisers preprocess and engineer features from the collected data to create meaningful predictors for the predictive model. These features may include user demographics, past behavior, content preferences, device information, geographic location, and temporal patterns.

3. Model Selection: Advertisers choose appropriate machine learning algorithms based on the nature of the data and the business objectives. Common predictive modeling techniques include logistic regression, decision trees, random forests, gradient boosting, neural networks, and deep learning models.

4. Training and Validation: Advertisers split the data into training and validation sets and train the predictive model using historical data. The model learns patterns and relationships in the data to make accurate predictions about user behavior and intent. Validation ensures that the model generalizes well to unseen data and performs reliably in real-world scenarios.

5. Prediction Generation: Once trained, the predictive model generates predictions about user behavior and intent in real time. Advertisers use these predictions to tailor ad targeting and messaging strategies, delivering personalized experiences that resonate with their target audience.

6. Iterative Improvement: Advertisers continuously monitor and evaluate the performance of the predictive model over time. They refine the model based on feedback and performance metrics, adjusting parameters, updating features, and incorporating new data sources to improve predictive accuracy and relevance.

Benefits:
Predictive analytics for audience insights and trends offer several key benefits for advertisers:

1. Enhanced Ad Targeting: By predicting user behavior and intent, advertisers can target their ads more effectively to users who are most likely to be interested in their products or services, maximizing ad relevance and engagement.

2. Improved Campaign Performance: Predictive analytics enables advertisers to optimize ad messaging and creative assets based on anticipated user actions, leading to higher click-through rates, conversion rates, and return on investment (ROI) for their campaigns.

3. Personalized User Experiences: By delivering personalized ad experiences tailored to individual preferences and intent, advertisers can enhance user satisfaction and loyalty, fostering deeper connections with their target audience.

4. Better Resource Allocation: Predictive analytics helps advertisers allocate budget and resources more efficiently, focusing investment on campaigns and channels with the highest predicted ROI and potential for success.

Case Example:
Consider an e-commerce retailer planning a promotional campaign for an upcoming sale event. Using predictive analytics, the retailer analyzes historical purchase data, website interactions, and demographic information to predict user behavior and intent.

Based on these predictions, the retailer tailors its ad targeting and messaging strategies to reach users who are most likely to purchase the sale event. For example, the retailer may target users who have previously shown interest in similar products or have a history of making purchases during promotional periods.

As a result, the retailer's campaign achieves higher conversion rates and sales volume compared to generic targeting strategies, demonstrating the effectiveness of predictive analytics in driving campaign success.

Conclusion:
Predictive analytics for audience insights and trends empower advertisers to anticipate user behavior and intent, enabling them to create personalized ad experiences that resonate with their target audience. By leveraging machine learning models to analyze historical data and contextual signals, advertisers can optimize ad targeting and messaging strategies, leading to improved campaign performance and user satisfaction. As the digital advertising landscape continues to evolve, predictive analytics will remain a valuable tool for advertisers seeking to stay ahead of the curve and drive business growth.

Case Study 10: Trend Analysis and Forecasting in Digital Advertising Markets

In the dynamic landscape of digital advertising, staying abreast of market trends and forecasting future demand is crucial for advertisers to maintain a competitive edge. Predictive analytics offers a powerful toolset to analyze market trends and anticipate shifts in consumer behavior, enabling advertisers to adapt their strategies proactively. In this case study, we explore how advertisers utilize predictive analytics for trend analysis and forecasting in digital advertising markets.

Background:
Digital advertising markets are characterized by rapid changes driven by technological advancements, shifts in consumer behavior, and evolving industry dynamics. Advertisers need to monitor these trends closely to identify emerging opportunities and threats, make informed decisions, and stay ahead of the competition. Predictive analytics enables advertisers to analyze historical data, identify patterns, and forecast future trends, providing valuable insights to guide strategic planning and execution.

Implementation:
The implementation of trend analysis and forecasting in digital advertising markets involves the following steps:

1. Data Collection: Advertisers collect a wide range of data sources, including historical performance data, market research reports, competitor analysis, consumer surveys, and industry news. This data encompasses key metrics such as ad spend, impressions, click-through rates, conversion rates, and demographic information.

2. Trend Identification: Advertisers use data visualization techniques and statistical analysis to identify trends and patterns in the collected data. They look for recurring patterns, seasonality effects, and long-term trends that may impact the digital advertising market.

3. Predictive Modeling: Advertisers deploy predictive analytics models to forecast future demand and market trends based on historical data and contextual factors. These models may include time series analysis, regression analysis, machine learning algorithms, and econometric models.

4. Scenario Planning: Advertisers conduct scenario planning exercises to assess the potential impact of different future scenarios on their advertising strategies. They model various scenarios, such as changes in consumer behavior, shifts in market dynamics, regulatory changes, and technological disruptions, to identify risks and opportunities.

5. Strategic Decision Making: Armed with insights from trend analysis and forecasting, advertisers make strategic decisions to optimize their advertising strategies and allocation of resources. They adjust budget allocations, media mix, messaging strategies, and targeting parameters to capitalize on emerging opportunities and mitigate potential risks.

Benefits:
Trend analysis and forecasting in digital advertising markets offer several key benefits for advertisers:

1. Strategic Planning: By analyzing market trends and forecasting future demand, advertisers can develop informed strategic plans to guide their advertising initiatives and investments.

2. Competitive Advantage: Predictive analytics enables advertisers to stay ahead of the competition by identifying emerging opportunities and threats in the digital advertising market and adapting their strategies accordingly.

3. Optimized Resource Allocation: Advertisers can allocate budget and resources more effectively by focusing investment on channels, audiences, and campaigns with the highest predicted ROI and potential for success.

4. Risk Mitigation: Trend analysis and forecasting help advertisers anticipate risks and uncertainties in the digital advertising market, allowing them to implement proactive measures to mitigate potential impacts on their business.
Case Example:
Consider a digital advertising agency planning a campaign for a client in the e-commerce industry. Using predictive analytics, the agency analyzes historical performance data, market trends, and consumer behavior to forecast future demand for the client's products.
Based on trend analysis and forecasting, the agency identifies emerging trends such as increasing demand for online shopping, growing interest in sustainable products, and rising adoption of mobile commerce. Armed with these insights, the agency develops a targeted advertising strategy that emphasizes mobile-friendly ad formats, highlights the client's sustainability initiatives, and leverages data-driven targeting to reach relevant audiences.

As a result, the client's campaign achieves higher engagement, conversion rates, and return on ad spend (ROAS) compared to previous campaigns, demonstrating the effectiveness of trend analysis and forecasting in driving campaign success.

Conclusion:
Trend analysis and forecasting in digital advertising markets empower advertisers to anticipate shifts in consumer behavior, identify emerging opportunities, and make informed strategic decisions. By leveraging predictive analytics to analyze historical data and contextual factors, advertisers can optimize their advertising strategies, allocate resources more effectively, and stay ahead of the competition in the fast-paced digital advertising landscape. As the industry continues to evolve, trend analysis and forecasting will remain essential tools for advertisers seeking to navigate uncertainties and capitalize on emerging trends.

VOICE AND VISUAL SEARCH ADVERTISING

Case Study 11: Implementing Voice Search Optimization Strategies with AI Technologies

As voice search becomes increasingly prevalent in our daily lives, advertisers are faced with the challenge of optimizing their ad campaigns to align with this emerging trend. Leveraging AI technologies, advertisers can implement voice search optimization strategies to ensure their ads are visible and engaging in voice-enabled search environments. In this case study, we delve into how advertisers harness AI to optimize their ad campaigns for voice search.

Background:
Voice search has revolutionized the way users interact with search engines, smart devices, and digital assistants. Instead

of typing queries into a search bar, users now use natural language commands to perform searches, ask questions, and seek information. Advertisers need to adapt their advertising strategies to accommodate this shift in user behavior and ensure their ads are optimized for voice search queries.

Implementation:
The implementation of voice search optimization strategies with AI technologies involves the following steps:

1. Natural Language Processing (NLP): Advertisers leverage NLP algorithms to understand the intent and context behind voice search queries. NLP algorithms analyze the structure and semantics of natural language queries to extract relevant keywords, entities, and user intent.

2. Keyword Research and Optimization: Advertisers conduct keyword research specifically tailored to voice search queries. They identify long-tail keywords, conversational phrases, and question-based queries commonly used in voice search interactions. Advertisers then optimize their ad content to include these voice search keywords and phrases.

3. Ad Content Creation: Advertisers create ad content that is conversational, concise, and relevant to voice search queries. They craft ad copy that directly addresses user questions, provides informative answers, and aligns with the user's intent. Advertisers also optimize ad headlines, descriptions, and calls to action for voice search compatibility.

4. Structured Data Markup: Advertisers implement structured data markup, such as schema.org markup, to provide search engines with additional context about their ad content. Structured data markup helps search engines understand the meaning and relevance of ad content, improving visibility and relevance in voice search results.

5. Voice Search Ad Targeting: Advertisers refine their ad targeting parameters to reach users who are likely to engage with voice search queries. They target audiences based on demographic information, location, device type, and search history, ensuring their ads are displayed to users performing voice searches on compatible devices.

6. Performance Monitoring and Optimization: Advertisers continuously monitor the performance of their voice search campaigns and optimize their strategies based on real-time data insights. They analyze key performance metrics such as impression share, click-through rate (CTR), conversion rate, and return on ad spend (ROAS) to refine targeting, ad content, and bidding strategies.

Benefits:
Implementing voice search optimization strategies with AI technologies offers several key benefits for advertisers:

1. Improved Visibility: By optimizing ad content for voice search queries, advertisers increase the visibility of their ads in voice-enabled search environments, ensuring they are displayed prominently in relevant search results.

2. Enhanced User Engagement: Advertisers provide users with relevant and informative ad content that directly addresses their voice search queries, resulting in higher engagement and interaction rates with ad campaigns.

3. Increased Relevance: Voice search optimization ensures ad content is tailored to user intent and context, making ads more relevant and meaningful to users performing voice searches.

4. Competitive Advantage: Advertisers gain a competitive edge by staying ahead of the curve and adapting their

advertising strategies to accommodate emerging trends in voice search technology.

Case Example:
Consider a retailer specializing in smart home devices launching a voice search advertising campaign for its latest product line. Leveraging AI technologies, the retailer optimizes its ad content to align with common voice search queries related to smart home automation, voice assistants, and connected devices.

The retailer creates ad copy that addresses user questions and provides detailed information about product features, compatibility, and use cases. Using structured data markup, the retailer enriches its ad content with additional context and metadata to improve visibility in voice search results.

As a result of these voice search optimization strategies, the retailer's ad campaigns achieve higher visibility, engagement, and conversion rates among users performing voice searches for smart home devices.

Conclusion:
Voice search optimization strategies powered by AI technologies enable advertisers to adapt their ad campaigns to the evolving landscape of voice-enabled search environments. By leveraging NLP algorithms, keyword research, structured data markup, and targeted ad strategies, advertisers can ensure their ads are visible, relevant, and engaging in voice search results. As voice search continues to gain momentum, advertisers must embrace these optimization strategies to maintain a competitive edge and effectively reach their target audience.

Case Study 12: Visual Recognition and Targeted Advertising in Image-Based Search Engines

In the era of visual-centric digital experiences, advertisers are exploring innovative ways to leverage visual recognition technology for targeted advertising. This case study delves into how advertisers harness visual recognition technology to analyze image content and context, enabling them to deliver highly relevant and contextually targeted ads in image-based search engines. By understanding visual cues and image attributes, advertisers can enhance ad targeting precision, driving higher engagement and conversion rates.

Background:
Image-based search engines have gained popularity as users increasingly rely on visual cues to search for information, products, and inspiration online. Advertisers recognize the potential of visual search as a powerful tool to connect with users in a visually engaging and contextually relevant manner. Visual recognition technology enables advertisers to analyze image content, identify objects, scenes, and attributes, and deliver targeted ads that align with user intent and preferences.

Implementation:
The implementation of visual recognition and targeted advertising in image-based search engines involves the following steps:

1. Image Analysis: Advertisers leverage visual recognition technology to analyze images uploaded by users in image-based search engines. Visual recognition algorithms analyze image content, detect objects, scenes, and visual attributes, and extract relevant features and metadata.

2. Keyword Extraction: Visual recognition algorithms extract keywords and descriptive metadata from images to understand the context and intent behind user searches. These keywords help advertisers identify relevant ad

targeting parameters and content themes that align with user interests and preferences.

3. Ad Content Matching: Advertisers match ad content with image attributes, context, and user intent to deliver highly relevant and contextually targeted ads. They create ad campaigns that align with the visual content of images and resonate with user preferences, enhancing ad relevance and engagement.

4. Contextual Targeting: Advertisers leverage contextual targeting parameters such as image content, context, user demographics, and browsing behavior to refine ad targeting and reach relevant audiences. They use machine learning algorithms to analyze user interactions and optimize ad delivery based on real-time feedback and performance data.

5. Performance Monitoring and Optimization: Advertisers monitor the performance of their visual recognition-based ad campaigns and optimize their strategies based on key performance indicators (KPIs) such as click-through rates (CTR), conversion rates, and return on ad spend (ROAS). They adjust ad targeting parameters, content themes, and bidding strategies to maximize campaign effectiveness and drive desired outcomes.

Benefits:
Visual recognition and targeted advertising in image-based search engines offer several key benefits for advertisers:

1. Enhanced Relevance: By analyzing image content and context, advertisers deliver highly relevant and contextually targeted ads that align with user intent and preferences, increasing ad relevance and engagement.

2. Improved User Experience: Visual recognition technology enhances the user experience by providing users with

visually engaging and contextually relevant ad content that meets their needs and interests.

3. Higher Engagement and Conversion Rates: Contextually targeted ads in image-based search engines drive higher engagement and conversion rates by delivering ads that resonate with user preferences and intent.

4. Optimized Ad Spend: Advertisers optimize ad targeting and content based on real-time performance data, maximizing the efficiency and effectiveness of ad spend and driving higher returns on investment (ROI).

Case Example:
Consider a fashion retailer launching a visual recognition-based ad campaign in an image-based search engine. Leveraging visual recognition technology, the retailer analyzes images uploaded by users to identify fashion trends, styles, and preferences.

The retailer creates ad content featuring products that match the visual attributes and context of images, such as clothing items, accessories, and footwear. Using contextual targeting parameters, the retailer delivers ads to users who are browsing images related to fashion, style inspiration, and outfit ideas.

As a result of these visual recognition-based targeting strategies, the retailer's ad campaign achieves higher engagement and conversion rates among users interested in fashion and style trends.

Conclusion:
Visual recognition and targeted advertising in image-based search engines enable advertisers to deliver highly relevant and contextually targeted ads that resonate with user intent and preferences. By leveraging visual recognition technology

to analyze image content and context, advertisers enhance ad relevance, engagement, and conversion rates. As visual search continues to gain traction, advertisers must embrace these innovative targeting strategies to effectively connect with users and drive business growth in the visual-centric digital landscape.

PRIVACY-PRESERVING AI SOLUTIONS

Case Study 13: Federated Learning Approaches for Privacy-Preserving Ad Targeting
In an era where data privacy concerns are paramount, advertisers are increasingly turning to privacy-preserving AI solutions to maintain user privacy while still harnessing the power of data-driven ad targeting. Federated learning is one such approach that allows advertisers to train machine learning models on decentralized data sources without compromising user privacy. In this case study, we delve into how advertisers leverage federated learning to enhance ad targeting capabilities while prioritizing user privacy and data security.

Background:
Traditional ad targeting methods often rely on centralized data collection and analysis, raising concerns about user privacy and data misuse. Federated learning offers a decentralized approach to machine learning where models are trained collaboratively across multiple devices or data sources without sharing raw data. This allows advertisers to leverage insights from diverse data sources while preserving user privacy and data sovereignty.

Implementation:
The implementation of federated learning approaches for privacy-preserving ad targeting involves the following steps:

1. Decentralized Training: Advertisers deploy machine learning models on decentralized data sources such as user devices, edge servers, or data centers. Each data source retains control over its data and participates in model training by computing model updates locally based on its own data.

2. Model Aggregation: Model updates from individual data sources are aggregated or averaged to generate a global model update. Federated learning algorithms ensure that model aggregation is performed in a privacy-preserving manner, without exposing raw data or individual user information.

3. Secure Model Exchange: Advertisers exchange model updates between data sources and a central server using secure communication protocols such as encryption and differential privacy. This ensures that model updates are transmitted securely and remain protected from unauthorized access or interception.

4. Iterative Model Refinement: The global model update is iteratively refined through multiple rounds of federated learning. Advertisers fine-tune model parameters based on aggregated feedback from decentralized data sources, gradually improving the model's accuracy and effectiveness for ad targeting.

5. Privacy-Preserving Analysis: Advertisers analyze insights and patterns derived from federated learning models without accessing raw data or individual user information. Aggregated model updates contain valuable insights about user preferences and behavior while preserving user privacy and data confidentiality.

Benefits:
Federated learning approaches for privacy-preserving ad targeting offer several key benefits for advertisers:

1. User Privacy Protection: By training machine learning models on decentralized data sources, advertisers protect user privacy and prevent sensitive data from being exposed to third parties or centralized servers.

2. Data Security: Federated learning ensures that raw data remains localized and secure within individual data sources, reducing the risk of data breaches, unauthorized access, or misuse.

3. Improved Ad Targeting: Advertisers leverage insights from federated learning models to enhance ad targeting capabilities and deliver more relevant and personalized ads to users, improving engagement and conversion rates.

4. Regulatory Compliance: Federated learning aligns with data privacy regulations such as GDPR and CCPA by minimizing data collection, sharing, and processing while still enabling data-driven ad targeting.

Case Example:
Consider a mobile app developer seeking to improve ad targeting capabilities while respecting user privacy. The developer implements federated learning techniques to train machine learning models on data collected from individual user devices.

Through federated learning, the developer aggregates insights from diverse user interactions with the app, such as app usage patterns, preferences, and interactions with ad content. By analyzing aggregated model updates, the developer gains valuable insights into user behavior and preferences without compromising user privacy.

As a result, the developer can enhance ad targeting capabilities and deliver more personalized and relevant ads to users, driving higher engagement and ad revenue without compromising user privacy.

Conclusion:
Federated learning approaches offer a promising solution for advertisers seeking to balance the benefits of data-driven ad targeting with the imperative to protect user privacy. By leveraging federated learning techniques, advertisers can train machine learning models on decentralized data sources, enhance ad targeting capabilities, and improve user engagement while preserving user privacy and data security. As privacy concerns continue to shape the digital advertising landscape, federated learning represents a forward-thinking approach to privacy-preserving AI solutions in ad targeting and beyond.

Case Study 14: Differential Privacy Techniques for Data Anonymization in AdTech Platforms
In the realm of AdTech platforms, preserving user privacy while extracting valuable insights for ad targeting and optimization is paramount. Differential privacy techniques offer a robust solution by anonymizing user data through the addition of noise to query results and statistical aggregates. This case study explores how advertisers leverage differential privacy techniques to safeguard user privacy in AdTech platforms while still deriving actionable insights for effective ad targeting and optimization.

Background:
AdTech platforms rely heavily on user data to deliver targeted ads, optimize campaigns, and measure ad performance. However, the collection and processing of user data raise concerns about privacy infringement and data misuse. Differential privacy provides a framework for quantifying the privacy guarantees of data analysis algorithms, ensuring that individual user identities remain confidential while still allowing for meaningful analysis and insights extraction.

Implementation:

The implementation of differential privacy techniques for data anonymization in AdTech platforms involves the following steps:

1. Noise Injection: Advertisers introduce controlled amounts of noise to query results and statistical aggregates derived from user data. This noise serves to obfuscate individual user contributions to the data while preserving the overall statistical properties of the dataset.

2. Privacy Budget Management: Advertisers allocate a privacy budget that determines the maximum allowable amount of noise that can be added to query results. The privacy budget reflects the level of privacy protection desired by advertisers and users and must be carefully managed to balance privacy guarantees with the utility of the data.

3. Aggregation of Noisy Data: Advertisers aggregate noisy data from multiple sources or queries to derive insights for ad targeting and optimization. Differential privacy ensures that the aggregated results maintain privacy guarantees, even when combining data from disparate sources or queries.

4. Query Optimization: Advertisers optimize query formulations and data processing pipelines to minimize the amount of noise required to achieve the desired level of privacy protection. By carefully structuring queries and aggregations, advertisers can maximize the utility of the data while minimizing privacy risks.

5. Privacy-Preserving Analysis: Advertisers analyze aggregated data with noise to extract insights for ad targeting, campaign optimization, and performance measurement. Differential privacy ensures that individual user identities remain confidential, even when conducting detailed analyses of user behavior and preferences.

Benefits:
Differential privacy techniques for data anonymization in AdTech platforms offer several key benefits for advertisers and users alike:

1. User Privacy Protection: By adding noise to query results and statistical aggregates, advertisers safeguard user privacy and prevent the disclosure of sensitive information or individual user identities.

2. Compliance with Regulations: Differential privacy techniques align with data privacy regulations such as GDPR and CCPA by ensuring that user data is anonymized and protected against unauthorized access or misuse.

3. Meaningful Analysis and Insights: Advertisers can still derive actionable insights from anonymized data for ad targeting, optimization, and performance measurement, enabling informed decision-making and campaign refinement.

4. Enhanced User Trust: By prioritizing user privacy and implementing robust privacy-preserving techniques, advertisers build trust and credibility with users, fostering positive relationships and brand loyalty.

Case Example:
Consider an AdTech platform seeking to improve ad targeting capabilities while upholding user privacy standards. The platform implements differential privacy techniques to anonymize user data collected from various sources, including website visits, app interactions, and ad impressions.

Through the addition of noise to query results and statistical aggregates, the platform ensures that individual user identities remain confidential while still allowing advertisers to derive valuable insights for targeted ad campaigns.

Advertisers can analyze anonymized data to identify audience segments, measure ad performance, and optimize campaign strategies without compromising user privacy.

As a result, the AdTech platform enhances its ad targeting capabilities, improves campaign effectiveness, and maintains user trust and privacy compliance.

Conclusion:
Differential privacy techniques offer a robust solution for protecting user privacy in AdTech platforms while still enabling meaningful analysis and insights extraction for ad targeting and optimization. By implementing differential privacy techniques, advertisers can balance the competing demands of privacy protection and data utility, fostering trust with users and ensuring compliance with regulatory requirements. As privacy concerns continue to shape the AdTech landscape, the adoption of differential privacy techniques represents a proactive approach to safeguarding user privacy and promoting responsible data practices in the digital advertising ecosystem.

ETHICAL CONSIDERATIONS AND RESPONSIBLE AI PRACTICES IN ADTECH

Case Study 15: Ensuring Fairness and Transparency in AI-Driven Ad Targeting

In the realm of AdTech, the ethical considerations surrounding AI-driven ad targeting practices are paramount. Advertisers must ensure that their algorithms are fair, transparent, and free from bias to maintain user trust and compliance with regulatory requirements. This case study delves into how advertisers audit algorithms for bias and discrimination to mitigate the risk of unintended consequences and uphold ethical standards in ad targeting.

Background:
AI-driven ad targeting relies on complex algorithms to analyze user data and deliver personalized ads. However, these algorithms can inadvertently perpetuate bias and discrimination, leading to unfair or discriminatory ad-targeting practices. Advertisers must proactively address these ethical concerns to protect user rights, maintain trust, and comply with regulations such as GDPR and anti-discrimination laws.

Implementation:
The implementation of ethical considerations and responsible AI practices in ad targeting involves the following steps:

1. Algorithm Auditing: Advertisers conduct regular audits of their AI algorithms to identify potential biases or discriminatory patterns. This involves analyzing historical data, model parameters, and decision-making processes to uncover instances of bias or unfairness.

2. Bias Detection and Mitigation: Advertisers use specialized tools and techniques to detect and mitigate bias in AI algorithms. This may include adjusting training data, refining model architectures, or implementing fairness-aware learning techniques to promote equity and fairness in ad targeting.

3. Transparency and Explainability: Advertisers prioritize transparency and explainability in AI-driven ad targeting practices to foster user trust and accountability. They provide clear explanations of how algorithms make ad targeting decisions and ensure that users have visibility into the data used and the factors influencing ad delivery.

4. User Consent and Control: Advertisers empower users with control over their data and ad preferences, allowing them to opt out of targeted advertising or adjust their ad settings as desired. User consent is central to ethical ad targeting

practices, and advertisers must respect user preferences and choices regarding data usage and ad personalization.

5. Regulatory Compliance: Advertisers adhere to regulatory requirements and industry standards governing data privacy, anti-discrimination, and consumer protection. They ensure that their ad targeting practices comply with laws such as GDPR, CCPA, and the Fair Housing Act to avoid legal liabilities and reputational damage.

Benefits:
Ensuring fairness and transparency in AI-driven ad targeting practices offers several key benefits for advertisers and users alike:

1. User Trust and Engagement: By prioritizing fairness and transparency, advertisers build trust with users and enhance engagement with targeted ads. Users are more likely to interact with ads that they perceive as fair, relevant, and respectful of their rights and preferences.
2. Compliance and Risk Mitigation: Advertisers mitigate legal and reputational risks by adhering to regulatory requirements and industry standards governing ad targeting practices. Compliance with laws such as GDPR and anti-discrimination statutes protects advertisers from fines, lawsuits, and brand damage associated with unethical or discriminatory practices.

3. Brand Reputation and Integrity: Ethical ad targeting practices contribute to a positive brand image and reputation. Advertisers that prioritize fairness, transparency, and user rights demonstrate a commitment to ethical values and responsible data practices, fostering goodwill and loyalty among users and stakeholders.

4. Social Responsibility: Ethical ad targeting practices align with corporate social responsibility initiatives and ethical business practices. Advertisers play a proactive role in

promoting fairness, equity, and inclusivity in digital advertising, contributing to a more ethical and sustainable advertising ecosystem.

Case Example:
Consider an online retailer implementing AI-driven ad targeting to promote its products to a diverse audience. Concerned about potential biases in its ad targeting algorithms, the retailer conducts a comprehensive audit of its AI models to identify and mitigate bias.

Through rigorous analysis of historical data and model parameters, the retailer uncovers instances of demographic bias in ad delivery, where certain demographic groups are disproportionately targeted or excluded from ad campaigns. To address this bias, the retailer adjusts its training data, fine-tunes its algorithms, and implements fairness-aware learning techniques to promote equitable ad targeting.

As a result of these efforts, the retailer enhances the fairness and transparency of its ad targeting practices, ensuring that all users have equal opportunities to engage with its ads regardless of demographic characteristics. Users perceive the retailer as a responsible and ethical advertiser, leading to increased trust, engagement, and brand loyalty.

Conclusion:
Ensuring fairness and transparency in AI-driven ad targeting practices is essential for maintaining user trust, compliance with regulations, and ethical integrity in the AdTech industry. By auditing algorithms for bias, promoting transparency and user control, and prioritizing regulatory compliance, advertisers can uphold ethical standards and promote fairness, equity, and inclusivity in digital advertising. As ethical considerations continue to shape the AdTech landscape, responsible AI practices represent a proactive approach to

building trust, mitigating risks, and fostering a more ethical and sustainable advertising ecosystem.

Case Study 16: Adhering to Ethical Guidelines and Regulatory Compliance in AdTech
In the rapidly evolving landscape of AdTech, ethical considerations and regulatory compliance are of utmost importance. Advertisers must navigate complex data governance frameworks and adhere to ethical guidelines to ensure that their ad targeting practices are transparent, fair, and compliant with relevant regulations. This case study explores how advertisers implement robust data governance and compliance frameworks to uphold ethical standards and regulatory requirements in AdTech.

Background:
AdTech platforms rely on vast amounts of user data to deliver targeted ads and optimize campaign performance. However, the collection, processing, and utilization of this data raise concerns about privacy infringement, data misuse, and discriminatory practices. Advertisers must proactively address these ethical considerations and comply with regulations such as GDPR (General Data Protection Regulation) and CCPA (California Consumer Privacy Act) to protect user rights, mitigate legal risks, and foster trust with users.

Implementation:
The implementation of ethical guidelines and regulatory compliance in AdTech involves the following key components:

1. Data Governance Framework: Advertisers establish robust data governance frameworks to govern the collection, storage, processing, and sharing of user data. This framework outlines policies, procedures, and controls to ensure that data handling practices align with ethical standards, industry best practices, and regulatory requirements.

2. Privacy by Design: Advertisers integrate privacy considerations into the design and development of AdTech platforms and products. They implement privacy-enhancing technologies, such as encryption, anonymization, and pseudonymization, to protect user data and minimize the risk of privacy breaches or unauthorized access.

3. User Consent and Transparency: Advertisers prioritize transparency and user consent in ad targeting practices. They provide clear and accessible privacy notices that inform users about data collection practices, purposes, and rights. Advertisers obtain explicit consent from users before collecting or processing personal data for ad targeting purposes.

4. Data Minimization and Purpose Limitation: Advertisers practice data minimization and purpose limitation to reduce the amount of data collected and processed to only what is necessary for ad targeting purposes. They refrain from collecting excessive or irrelevant data and ensure that data is used solely for specified and legitimate purposes.

5. Regulatory Compliance: Advertisers comply with regulatory requirements such as GDPR and CCPA by implementing measures to protect user privacy and rights. They appoint data protection officers, conduct privacy impact assessments, and maintain records of data processing activities to demonstrate compliance with legal obligations.

Benefits:
Adhering to ethical guidelines and regulatory compliance in AdTech offers several key benefits for advertisers and users:

1. User Trust and Confidence: By prioritizing ethical standards and regulatory compliance, advertisers build trust and confidence with users. Users are more likely to engage with

ads and share their data with advertisers they perceive as ethical, transparent, and respectful of their privacy rights.

2. Legal and Reputational Protection: Advertisers mitigate legal risks and reputational damage by complying with regulations such as GDPR and CCPA. Compliance with data protection laws safeguards advertisers from fines, penalties, and lawsuits associated with privacy violations or data breaches.

3. Competitive Advantage: Ethical advertising practices can serve as a competitive differentiator for advertisers. Companies that prioritize user privacy and adhere to ethical guidelines gain a competitive edge by distinguishing themselves as trustworthy and responsible stewards of user data.

4. Long-Term Sustainability: Advertisers contribute to the long-term sustainability of the AdTech ecosystem by promoting ethical standards and responsible data practices. Ethical advertising practices foster a culture of trust, integrity, and accountability, driving positive outcomes for advertisers, users, and the broader digital advertising industry.

Case Example:
Consider a digital advertising agency seeking to enhance its ad targeting capabilities while maintaining compliance with privacy regulations. The agency implements a comprehensive data governance framework that encompasses policies, procedures, and controls to ensure ethical ad-targeting practices and regulatory compliance.

Through the adoption of privacy by design principles, the agency integrates privacy considerations into its ad-targeting platforms and products. It implements user consent mechanisms, provides transparent privacy notices, and practices data minimization and purpose limitation to protect user privacy and rights.

As a result of these efforts, the agency builds trust and credibility with clients and users alike. Clients trust the agency to handle their data responsibly and comply with legal requirements, while users feel confident that their privacy rights are respected and protected. The agency gains a competitive advantage in the market by demonstrating its commitment to ethical advertising practices and regulatory compliance.

Conclusion:
Adhering to ethical guidelines and regulatory compliance is essential for maintaining trust, integrity, and accountability in the AdTech industry. By implementing robust data governance frameworks, practicing privacy by design principles, obtaining user consent, and complying with regulations such as GDPR and CCPA, advertisers can uphold ethical standards, protect user privacy, and foster a culture of trust and transparency in ad targeting practices. As ethical considerations continue to shape the AdTech landscape, responsible data practices represent a strategic imperative for advertisers seeking to build sustainable, ethical, and trusted relationships with users and stakeholders.

APPENDIX

In this appendix, we provide a curated list of resources and tools to help AdTech professionals stay informed, enhance their skills, and succeed in the rapidly evolving landscape of digital advertising. From recommended books and articles to useful tools and software, as well as online courses and training programs, this appendix serves as a comprehensive guide for professionals looking to deepen their knowledge and expertise in AdTech.

RECOMMENDED BOOKS

1. "Ad Serving Technology: Understand the Marketing Revelation That Commercialized the Internet" by Gregory Cristal
2. "The Adweek Copywriting Handbook: The Ultimate Guide to Writing Powerful Advertising and Marketing Copy" by Joseph Sugarman
3. "Data-Driven Marketing: The 15 Metrics Everyone in Marketing Should Know" by Mark Jeffery
4. "Hooked: How to Build Habit-Forming Products" by Nir Eyal
5. "Programmatic Advertising: The Successful Transformation to Automated, Data-Driven Marketing in Real-Time" by Oliver Busch

RECOMMENDED ARTICLES

1. AdExchanger - A leading source for news, analysis, and insights on programmatic advertising and digital marketing.
2. Marketing Land - Offers in-depth articles, how-to guides, and industry updates on all aspects of digital marketing, including AdTech.
3. AdAge - Provides breaking news, analysis, and commentary on advertising and marketing trends, including insights into AdTech innovations.

4. Think with Google - Offers research, case studies, and best practices for digital marketers, with a focus on data-driven advertising strategies.
5. AdTech Weekly - A curated newsletter featuring the latest news, trends, and insights from the AdTech industry.

USEFUL TOOLS & SOFTWARE

1. Google Ads - A powerful advertising platform for creating, managing, and optimizing digital ad campaigns across various channels, including search, display, and video.
2. Facebook Ads Manager - Allows advertisers to create, manage, and analyze ad campaigns on Facebook, Instagram, Messenger, and Audience Network.
3. Adobe Advertising Cloud - An end-to-end platform for planning, executing, and optimizing advertising campaigns across multiple channels and formats.
4. SEMrush - Offers a suite of tools for competitive analysis, keyword research, and campaign optimization in search engine marketing (SEM).
5. Optimizely - A leading experimentation platform that enables advertisers to A/B test ad creatives, landing pages, and user experiences to optimize campaign performance.

ONLINE COURSES & TRAINING PROGRAMS

1. Coursera - Offers a wide range of courses and specializations in AI, ML, and data science, including topics relevant to AdTech such as predictive analytics and machine learning for marketing.
2. Udacity - Provides nano degree programs in data science, machine learning, and AI, with hands-on projects and real-world applications in digital advertising.
3. edX - Offers courses from top universities and institutions in AI, ML, and data science, covering topics such as natural language processing, image recognition, and customer segmentation for AdTech.

4. DataCamp - Specializes in data science and analytics training, with courses and tutorials on programming languages like Python and R, as well as machine learning techniques for AdTech professionals.

5. LinkedIn Learning - Provides video-based courses on a variety of topics, including AI, ML, and data science, with practical examples and case studies relevant to AdTech applications.

In conclusion, the resources and tools listed in this appendix offer AdTech professionals valuable insights, practical knowledge, and hands-on skills to navigate the complexities of digital advertising and drive business growth in an increasingly data-driven and technology-driven environment. By investing in continuous learning and staying abreast of industry trends, professionals can position themselves for success and make meaningful contributions to the future of AdTech.

www.ingramcontent.com/pod-product-compliance
Lightning Source LLC
LaVergne TN
LVHW051344050326
832903LV00031B/3725